EK   H
SAN JOSE PUBLIC LIBRARY (16)   3-25-91   8

D0607142

Great Passenger Ships of the World

Volume 4: 1936 – 1950

Dunnottar Castle

Great Passenger Ships of the World

Volume 4: 1936 – 1950

Arnold Kludas

Translated by Charles Hodges

387.2432
T tt

7/86

Patrick Stephens, Wellingborough

© Copyright 1972-1974 Gerhard Stalling Verlag,
Oldenburg/Hamburg
© Copyright 1977 Patrick Stephens Limited

All rights reserved. No part of this publication may be
reproduced, stored in a retrieval system or transmitted,
in any form or by any means, electronic, mechanical,
photocopying, recording or otherwise, without prior
permission in writing from the publishers.

First published in Germany under the title *Die Grossen
Passagierschiffe der Welt*
First published in Great Britain—1977
Reprinted May 1985

British Library Cataloguing in Publication Data

Kludas, Arnold
   Great passenger ships of the world.
   Vol. 4 : 1936-1950
   1. Passenger ships—History—Pictorial works
   I. Title   II. Die grossen Passagierschiffe
   der Welt. *English*
   387.2'43'09034   VM381

   ISBN 0-85059-253-4

*Patrick Stephens Limited is part of the
Thorsons Publishing Group.*

Text filmset in 10 on 12 pt English 49 by
Stevenage Printing Limited, Stevenage.
Printed in Great Britain on 100 gsm Fineblade coated
cartridge, and bound, by The Garden City Press,
Letchworth, Herts, for the publishers Patrick Stephens
Limited, Denington Estate, Wellingborough,
Northants, NN8 2QD, England.

Foreword

This volume—the fourth in the series— deals with developments during the 15 years from 1936 to 1950, a period that saw the last, highly interesting, pre-war tonnage which was intended to be placed in service on all routes following the lifting of the world-wide depression of the early '30s. Among the largest passenger ships built during the years under review were the Queen Elizabeth and the Wilhelm Gustloff, the latter the first to be commissioned expressly for cruising on present-day lines. Many of the ships which were on the stocks when hostilities broke out were either never completed or were converted for war service. The standard types produced by the Americans for use as troop transports take up nearly a third of this volume. New passenger liners were laid down at the end of the war and by 1950 were on world-wide service alongside pre-war veterans. It was not then fully appreciated in shipping company board rooms that the principal routes were by this time being served by another means of transport, namely the aeroplane, whose development had been accelerated by the pressing needs of war. It was not regarded as an immediate threat but rather as a competitor which would take only a small percentage of the market.

In the recording of these significant events in the history of passenger shipping I have had the selfless assistance of Mr N.R.P. Bonsor of Jersey, who read through my manuscript and added and corrected many details, and also Mr Frank O. Braynard of Sea Cliff and Mr Paul H. Silverstone of New York, without whose willing help it would have been practically impossible to illustrate the section on United States troopships.

Arnold Kludas

Hamburg: July, 1976.

Explanatory Notes

All passenger ships ever launched having a gross registered tonnage (GRT) of over 10,000 are presented in the five volumes of this work. This fourth volume deals with the period 1936 to 1950. The ships are arranged chronologically, with the exception of sister-ships or groups of ships which have been placed together regardless of exact chronology. The chronological order of the individual sections has been determined from the launching date of the first ship of the class or group. The technical/historical biography of each ship appears under the name with which the ship first entered service. This applies also if the ship sailed later under other names and for other shipping companies. This rule is departed from only in exceptional circumstances. To trace a particular ship the reader is recommended to use the Index of Ships' Names, pages 229/231. In cases where ships have been renamed these are included after the first name in each case, as a further help in tracing all the later names, each with the year of the name change. The following is a guide to the technical and historical information concerning the ships.

I. Technical Data
The information given in the paragraph on technical data applies fundamentally to the date when the ship first went into service as a passenger carrier. Planned specifications are given in the case of incomplete ships for which at their respective stages of construction these had not been fully decided upon. Alterations affecting technical data are noted with historical notes against the appropriate dates.

Dimensions Length overall × moulded breadth in metres rounded off to one place of decimals, followed by the equivalent in feet, the length to the nearest whole number and breadth to one place of decimals. Length overall has been adopted in preference to other length measurements. It was found that recorded registered length and length between perpendiculars could vary from time to time and from place to place.

Propulsion Type of machinery, constructor. Where the shipbuilder has not been responsible for the propelling machinery, its constructor is given. The abbreviations III or IV exp eng indicate triple or quadruple expansion (steam) engines.

Power The figure of horse power given is the highest performance attainable by the engines in normal service. The different methods of measuring horse power, according to the form of propulsion, are as follows:
IHP = indicated horse power, unit of measurement for reciprocating steam engines and internal combustion engines.
SHP = shaft horse power, unit of measurement for turbine machinery and internal combustion engines.
BHP = brake horse power, unit of measurement for internal combustion engines.
The horse power figures, thus arrived at through different methods, cannot necessarily be compared with each other. While BHP and SHP are practically identical, their relationship to the indicated horse power (IHP) is in the region of 4:5. 8,000 SHP is thus equivalent to 10,000 IHP.

Speed Service speed is given in knots. This is followed, as far as can be established, by the highest speed achieved on trials with the engines running at maximum power.

Passengers On nearly all ships the passenger accommodation and the number of berths for each class were frequently altered. Even if it were still possible today to establish all these changes exactly, the necessary effort would not justify the value of the figures thus obtained. One can come to completely different conclusions however correct the figures, for sofa-berths or emergency beds may or may not have been included. The information on alterations to passenger accommodation therefore is limited to really significant modifications, as far as it has been possible to determine them. The standard in the lowest-priced classes of passenger accommodation varied from ship to ship, and between owners and routes, from large mass dormitories (which could be used alternatively for the carriage of cargo) to relatively comfortably equipped rooms with a moderate number of beds. On many ships these variations existed side by side under the general description of 'third class'.

Crew Crew-strength also was subject to alteration, as for instance when a ship was converted from coal to oil-firing, or when the passenger capacity was changed. Changes in crew-strength have not been noted. Unfortunately it has not been possible to determine crew strength for every ship.

II. Historical Data
The historical information reflects in chronological order the career of the ship, giving all important events and facts.

Owners In the ships' biographies, shipowners are indicated throughout by what are considered to be the accepted short-forms in English-speaking countries. Nevertheless, a selected short-form may not itself be based on an English translation of a non-English title, for instance: Nippon Yusen KK, CGT, etc. It is assumed that Cie, Cia, AG, SA, etc, will be as familiar to readers as are such English abbreviations as SN, Co, Corp, etc. After the name of a shipowner, the location mentioned in each case is the ship's home port, which is not necessarily where the shipowner has his head office.
An alphabetical list of all shipowners with their complete styles is included as an appendix to Volume 5.

Contents

Builders Like shipowners, builders are noted throughout by their accepted short-forms, and are listed alphabetically with their complete styles in Volume 5.

Completion Completion-date is the date of commencement of trials.

Routes Ports of call are omitted from the information concerning routes. During the '30s the large liner companies offered cruising programmes of varying extent. Even the ships of the companies engaged on regular services were used for cruising as opportunity afforded.

The Strathmore Class

Turbine steamer *Strathmore*
P & O Line, London

1963 *Marianna Latsi*
1966 *Henrietta Latsi*

Builders: Vickers Armstrongs,
Barrow
Yard no: 698
23,428 GRT; 202.7 × 25.0 m /
665 × 82.0 ft; Parsons geared
turbines from builders; Twin
screw; 28,000 SHP; 20, max
22.28 kn; Passengers: 445 1st class,
665 tourist class; Crew: 515.

1935 Apr 4: Launched.
Sep: Completed.
Sep 27: Cruising from London to
the Canaries.
Oct 26: Maiden voyage London-
Sydney.
1939 The *Strathmore* became a
troop transport.
1948/49 Overhauled and refitted
after release from naval service.
Pasengers: 497 1st class, 487
tourist class. 23,580 GRT.
1949 Oct 27: First post-war voyage
London-Sydney.
1961 Sep: Only tourist class,
approximately 1,200 passengers.
1963 Sold to John S. Latsis,
Piraeus.
Renamed *Marianna Latsi*. Used
for pilgrim voyages in Asiatic
waters, and occasionally as a hotel
ship at Jeddah.
1966 Renamed *Henrietta Latsi*.
1967 Apr 18: Laid up at Eleusis.
1969 May 27: The *Henrietta Latsi*
arrived at La Spezia where she was
broken up.

Turbine steamer *Stratheden*
P & O Line, London

1964 *Henrietta Latsi*
1966 *Marianna Latsi*

Builders: Vickers Armstrongs,
Barrow
Yard no: 722
23,722 GRT; 202.3 × 25.0 m /
664 × 82.0 ft; Parsons geared
turbines from builders; Twin
screw; 28,000 SHP; 20, max
21.8 kn; passengers: 448 1st class,
563 tourist class; Crew: 563.

1937 Jun 10: Launched.
Dec 10: Completed.
Dec 24: Maiden voyage London-
Sydney.
1939 Troop transport.
1946 Released from naval service,
then overhauled and refitted by
Vickers Armstrongs. Passengers:
527 1st class, 453 tourist class.
23,732 GRT.
1947 Jun: First post-war voyage
London-Sydney.
1950 Four voyages Southampton-
New York under charter to
Cunard.
1961 Only tourist class,
approximately 1,200 passengers.
1964 Sold to John S. Latsis,
Piraeus.
Renamed *Henrietta Latsi*.
Used for pilgrim voyages in Asiatic
waters.
1966 Renamed *Marianna Latsi*.
1969 May 19: Arrived at La Spezia
to be broken up.

1 *A further development of the* Strath
ships of 1931, the Strathmore *entered
service in 1935.*
2 *The* Stratheden *sailed on her maiden
voyage in December 1937.*

Turbine steamer *Strathallan*
P & O Line, London

Builders: Vickers Armstrongs
Barrow
Yard no: 729
23,722 GRT; 203.5 × 25.0 m /
668 × 82.0 ft; Parsons geared
turbines from builders; Twin
screw; 28,000 SHP; 20 max 22 kn;
Passengers: 448 1st class, 563
tourist class; Crew: 563.

1937 Sep 23: Launched.
1938 Mar: Completed.
Mar 18: Maiden voyage London-
Sydney.
1939 Troop transport.
1942 Dec 21: While sailing in
convoy from Glasgow to Algiers the
Strathallan was torpedoed 40
nautical miles north of Oran by the
German submarine *U 562*. After
the 5,000 or so people on board had
been transferred to other ships, the
liner was taken in tow, but sank
the next morning in position
36° 52′N-00° 34′W. 11 dead.

3/4 The last ship in her class, the
Strathallan *entered service in 1938. In*
picture 4 she is shown as a troop
transport.

The Last Union-Castle Liners before 1939

Motorship *Stirling Castle*
Union-Castle Line, London

Builders: Harland & Wolff, Belfast
Yard no: 941
25,550 GRT; 221.0 × 25.0 m /
725 × 82.0 ft; Burmeister & Wain
diesels, H & W; Twin screw;
24,000 BHP; 20 kn; Passengers:
297 1st class, 492 cabin class.

1935 Aug 15: Launched.
1936 Jan: Completed.
Feb 7: Maiden voyage
Southampton-Cape Town.
1940 Troop transport.
1946 Released from naval service,
then overhauled and refitted by
Harland & Wolff. Passengers: 245
1st class, 538 tourist class. 25,554
GRT.
1947 Southampton-Cape Town
service again.
1966 Mar 3: Arrived at Mihara.
Broken up by Nichimen Co.

Motorship *Athlone Castle*
Union-Castle Line, London

Builders: Harland & Wolff, Belfast
Yard no: 942
25,564 GRT; 221.0 × 25.0 m /
725 × 82.0 ft; Burmeister & Wain
diesels, H & W; Twin screw;
24,000 BHP; 20 kn; Passengers:
242 1st class, 487 cabin class.

1935 Nov 28: Launched.
1936 May: Completed.
May 22: Maiden voyage
Southampton-Cape Town.
1939 Troop transport.
1946 Released from naval service,
then overhauled and refitted by
Harland & Wolff. Passengers: 245
1st class, 538 tourist class. 25,567
GRT.
1947 Re-entered Southampton-
Cape Town service.
1965 Sep 13: Arrived at
Kaohsiung.
Broken up by China Steel Corp.

1/3 The first ships of a new type, the sister ships Stirling Castle (*1*) *and* Athlone Castle (*2*) *entered service in 1935. Picture 3 shows the* Athlone Castle *as a troop transport.*

1

2

3

Motorship *Capetown Castle*
Union-Castle Line, London

Builders: Harland & Wolff, Belfast
Yard no: 986
27,002 GRT; 223.6 × 25.1 m /
734 × 82.3 ft; Burmeister & Wain
diesels, H & W; Twin screw;
28,000 BHP; 20 kn; Passengers:
292 1st class, 499 cabin class.

1937 Sep 23: Launched.
1938 Apr: Completed.
Apr 29: Maiden voyage
Southampton-Cape Town.
1939 Troop transport.
1946 Released from naval service,
then overhauled by Harland &
Wolff. Passengers: 243 1st class,
553 tourist class.
1947 Jan: First post-war voyage
Southampton-Cape Town.
1960 Oct 17: Seven crew members
were killed in an engine-room
explosion off Las Palmas.
1967 Sep 26: Arrived at La Spezia.
Broken up by Terrestre Marittima.

Motorship *Dunvegan Castle*
Union-Castle Line, London

Builders: Harland & Wolff, Belfast
Yard no: 960
15,007 GRT; 170.7 × 21.9 m /
560 × 71.9 ft; Burmeister & Wain
diesels, H & W; Twin screw;
11,200 BHP; 17 kn; Passengers:
258 1st class, 250 tourist class.

1936 Mar 26: Launched.
Aug 18: Completed.
Sep: Maiden voyage in London-
round Africa service.
1939 On the outbreak of war fitted
out as armed merchant cruiser.
1940 Aug 27: The *Dunvegan
Castle* was torpedoed west of
Ireland by the German submarine
U 46. She sank the following day in
position 55°N-11°W. 27 dead.

4 *The* Capetown Castle *was an
enlarged version of her two
predecessors.*
5 *Union-Castle Line built the sister
ships* Dunvegan Castle (5) *and*
Dunnottar Castle *for the round-Africa
service.*

Motorship *Dunnottar Castle*
Union-Castle Line, London

1959 *Victoria*

Builders: Harland & Wolff, Belfast
Yard no: 959
15,007 GRT; 170.7 × 21.9 m /
560 × 71.9 ft; Burmeister & Wain
diesels, H & W; Twin screw;
11,200 BHP; 17 kn; Passengers:
258 1st class, 250 tourist class.

1936 Jan 25: Launched.
Jun: Completed.
Jul: Maiden voyage Southampton-
Cape Town, then used in London-
round Africa service.
1939 Oct 14: Entered service as
armed merchant cruiser.
1942 Troop transport.
1948 Released from naval service.
15,054 GRT after overhaul.
Passengers: 105 1st class, 263
tourist class.
1949 Feb: First post-war voyage in
London-round Africa service.
1958 Sold to Incres SS Co,
Monrovia.
1959 Renamed *Victoria*.
Jan: The *Victoria* arrived at Wilton
Fijenoord, Rotterdam, where she
was completely rebuilt as a cruise
liner for 600 passengers, 1st class.
New FIAT diesel fitted with 16,800
BHP for 18, max 21 knots.
174.4 m / 572 ft length overall.
14,917 GRT.
Dec 14: First cruise after
rebuilding work.
1960 Jan 8: One voyage Le Havre-
New York, then used for New
York-West Indies cruises.
1964 Oct: Sold to the Victoria SS
Co, Monrovia, a subsidiary of the
Swedish shipping company A/B
Clipper. Continued in the same
service, with Incres acting as
agents.

1975 Nov: Sold to Phaidon Nav,
part of the Chandris group, and
registered under the Greek flag.
Dec 11: Arrived at Piraeus, towed
by the *Heidi Moran*.
1976 Jun 6: Left Piraeus.
Cruising.

6 *The* Dunnottar Castle.
7 *In 1959 the ship was completely rebuilt for the Incres Line and then used for cruising.*

Motorship *Durban Castle*
Union-Castle Line, London

Builders: Harland & Wolff, Belfast
Yard no: 987
17,388 GRT; 181.2 × 23.2 m /
594 × 76.1 ft; Burmeister & Wain
diesels, H & W; Twin screw;
17,000 BHP; 18.5 kn; Passengers:
220 1st class, 335 tourist class.

1938 Jun 14: Launched.
Nov 22: Completed.
Dec 15: Delivered.
Dec 31: Maiden voyage London-
Cape Town.
1940 Troop transport. Used as a
landing ship during the later years
of the war.
1947 Jul: Entered London-round
Africa service after overhaul.
17,382 GRT. Passengers: 180 1st
class, 359 tourist class.
1962 Broken up at Hamburg by
Eisen & Metall.

Motorship *Pretoria Castle*
Union-Castle Line, London

1946 *Warwick Castle*

Builders: Harland & Wolff, Belfast
Yard no: 1006
17,392 GRT; 181.2 × 23.2 m /
594 × 76.1 ft; Burmeister & Wain
diesels, H & W; Twin screw;
17,000 BHP; 18.5 kn; Passengers:
220 1st class, 335 tourist class.

1938 Oct 12: Launched.
1939 Apr: Completed.
Apr 20: Maiden voyage London-
round Africa.
Nov: Commissioned as armed
merchant cruiser.
1942/43 Converted to auxiliary
aircraft carrier.
1943 Mar 18: Entered service as
training ship.
1946 Re-converted to passenger
ship by Harland & Wolff at
Belfast. 17,387 GRT. Passengers:

180 1st class, 359 tourist class.
Renamed *Warwick Castle*.
1947 Mar: First post-war voyage
London-round Africa.
1962 Jul 26: Arrived at Barcelona
to be broken up.

8

8/9 *The Durban Castle in the year 1946 (8), and at the Hamburg shipbreaker's yard in 1962.*
10/11 *The Pretoria Castle served as an aircraft carrier (10) during the Second World War, and was then renamed Warwick Castle (11) in 1946.*

9

10

11

The Awatea

Turbine steamer *Awatea*
Union SS Co of New Zealand,
Wellington

Builders: Vickers-Armstrongs,
Barrow
Yard no: 707
13,482 GRT; 166.0 × 22.6 m /
545 × 74.1 ft; Geared turbines
from builders; Twin screw; 22,500
SHP; 22, max 23 kn; Passengers:
377 1st class, 151 tourist class, 38
3rd class.

1936 Feb 25: Launched.
Jul 25: Completed.
Aug 5: Left Birkenhead for
Wellington.
Sep 15: Maiden voyage Sydney-
Auckland.
1940 Several voyages Sydney-
Auckland-Vancouver until 1941.
1941 Sep: Entered service as troop
transport.
1942 The *Awatea* collided off
Halifax with a US destroyer, which
broke in two and sank.
Nov 11: The *Awatea* was attacked
and hit several times by German
bombers between Bougie and
Gibraltar. The ship had to be
abandoned and sank near Cape
Carbon.

1/2 The Awatea, *sunk in 1942 while
serving as a troop transport.*

1

2

Pretoria and Windhuk

Turbine steamer *Pretoria*
German East Africa Line,
Hamburg

1945 *Empire Doon*
1949 *Empire Orwell*
1959 *Gunung Djati*

Builders: Blohm & Voss, Hamburg
Yard no: 506
16,662 GRT; 176.0 × 22.1 m /
577 × 72.5 ft; Geared turbines,
B & V; Twin screw; 14,200 SHP;
18 kn; Passengers: 152 1st class,
338 tourist class; Crew: 263.

1936 Jul 16: Launched.
Dec 4: Completed.
Dec 12: Delivered.
Dec 19: Maiden voyage Hamburg-
Cape Town.
1939 Naval accommodation ship.
Later in service as hospital ship.
1945 Used in the evacuation of the
German eastern territories.
May: British war prize.
Oct: Taken over as *Empire Doon*
by the Ministry of Transport;
managed by Orient Line. 17,362
GRT.
1948/49 Engine alterations. New
boilers. Two of the eight turbines
removed. 10,000 SHP, 16 knots,
18,036 GRT.
1949 Renamed *Empire Orwell*.
1958 Chartered to the Pan Islamic
SS Co, Karachi.
Nov: Sold to Blue Funnel Line,
Liverpool. Refitted at Glasgow by
Barclay, Curle & Co. 17,891 GRT.
Passengers: 106 1st class, 2,000
3rd class.
1959 Mar: First voyage as the
Gunung Djati in the Indonesia-
Jeddah pilgrim service.
1962 Sold to the Indonesian
government.
1965 Sold to P.T. Maskapai
Pelajaran 'Sang Saka', Djakarta.

17,516 GRT.
1966 Sold again to P.T.
Perusahaan Pelajaran 'Arafat',
Djakarta. The *Gunung Djati*
continued in the Indonesia-Jeddah
service.
1973 Apr: Until October, refit at
Hongkong United Dockyards.
Geared turbines replaced by MAN
diesels. 12,000 BHP.

1/2 The German East Africa Line's
Pretoria *(1) sails today as the* Gunung
Djati *under the Indonesian flag.*

Turbine steamer *Windhuk*
Woermann Line, Hamburg

1943 *Lejeune*

Builders: Blohm & Voss, Hamburg
Yard no: 507
16,662 GRT; 175.8 × 22.1 m /
577 × 72.5 ft; Geared turbines,
B & V; Twin screw; 14,200 SHP;
18 kn; Passengers: 152 1st class,
338 tourist class; Crew: 263.

1936 Aug 27: Launched.
1937 Mar 10: Completed.
Apr 12: Maiden voyage Hamburg-
Cape Town.
1939 At the outbreak of war the
Windhuk was at Lobito.
On November 16 the ship sailed for
South America and reached Santos
on December 7. During the voyage
the *Windhuk* was disguised as the
Osaka Shosen liner *Santos Maru*.
1942 Jan 29: Seized by the
Brazilian government.
May 12: Sold to the US Navy.
1943 Mar 26: Commissioned as
the *Lejeune*.
1944 May 12: Accommodation for
4,660 troops after refit as transport
at Norfolk. Second funnel
removed.
1948 Feb 9: Laid up at Tacoma.
1957 Jul: Handed over to US
Maritime Commission. Still laid
up.
1966 Aug 16: To Portland to be
broken up by Zidell Explorations
Inc.

3/4 *The* Windhuk (3) *took refuge at
Santos in December 1939. Picture 4
shows her at Santos disguised as the*
Santos Maru.
5 *The* Lejeune *ex* Windhuk *in April
1945.*

3

4

5

The City of Benares

Turbine steamer *City of Benares*
Ellerman Lines, Glasgow

Builders: Barclay, Curle & Co,
Glasgow
Yard no: 656
11,081 GRT; 155.1 × 19.1 m /
509 × 62.7 ft; Geared turbines,
Cammell Laird; Single screw;
6,600 SHP; 15, max 17.25 kn;
Passengers: 219 in one class; Crew:
180.

1936 Aug 5: Launched.
Oct 15: Delivered.
Oct 24: Maiden voyage Liverpool-
Bombay.
1940 Sep 18: While on a voyage
from England to Canada the *City
of Benares* was torpedoed by the
German submarine *U 48* in
position 56° 43′N-21° 15′W. There
were 406 people on board,
including 90 children who were
being evacuated to Canada. The
City of Benares sank very quickly.
Due to the bad weather it was
extremely difficult to lower the
boats and 248 people died, 77 of
them children. (The torpedoing
took place on September 17 by
British time.)

1 *Ellerman liner* City of Benares, *built
in 1936.*

1

Turbine steamer *Nieuw Amsterdam*
Holland-America Line, Rotterdam

Builders: Rotterdamsche DD Mij
Yard no: 200
36,287 GRT; 231.2 × 26.8 m / 759 × 87.9 ft; Parsons geared turbines 'De Schelde'; Twin screw; 35,100 SHP; 20.5, max 22.8 kn; Passengers: 556 1st class, 455 tourist class, 209 3rd class; Crew: 694.

1937 Apr 10: Launched.
1938 Mar 21: Completed.
Apr 15: Delivered.
May 10: Maiden voyage Rotterdam-New York.
1939 Sep: Laid up at New York due to outbreak of war.
1940 Cruising from New York. After the German invasion of the Netherlands the *Nieuw Amsterdam* was placed at the disposal of the British Ministry of Transport.
Sep: Refitted at Halifax as transport with accommodation for 8,000 troops and placed in service under Cunard management.
1946 Apr 26: Arrived at Amsterdam for the first time after six years of war service.
Overhauled and refitted by builders.
1947 Oct 29: First post-war voyage Rotterdam-New York. Passengers: 552 1st class, 426 cabin class, 209 tourist class. 36,667 GRT.

1957 Grey hull.
1961 Alterations to passenger accommodation: 574 1st class, 583 tourist class. 36,982 GRT.
1967 Aug 16: New boilers fitted by Wilton-Fijenoord, the work lasting until the end of year.
1971 Dec: The *Nieuw Amsterdam* now used only for cruises.
1972 Registered at Willemstad for NV Nieuw Amsterdam.
1974 Jan: Sold to be broken up in Taiwan.

1 The *Nieuw Amsterdam*, *originally intended as* Prinsendam, *was for a long time the flagship of the Holland-America Line.*
2 *In 1957 the ship's hull was painted grey.*

1

2

Motorship *Noordam*
Holland-America Line, Rotterdam

1963 *Oceanien*

Builders: P. Smit jr, Rotterdam
Yard no: 515
10,704 GRT; 152.9 × 19.5 m /
502 × 64.0 ft; Burmeister & Wain
diesels, Smit; Twin screw; 13,000
BHP; 17, max 19.7 kn;
Passengers: 125 tourist class.

1938 Apr 9: Launched.
Sep 15: Completed.
Sep 28: Maiden voyage Rotterdam-
New York.
1940 Mar 14: First voyage New
York-Java.
1942 Apr: Taken over as transport
by the American War Shipping
Administration.
1946 Jul: First post-war voyage
Rotterdam-New York. Now 10,276
GRT. 148 1st class passengers.
1963 Sold to Cielomar SA,
Panama. Renamed *Oceanien*. The
name originally intended was
Wallisien. Chartered to
Messageries Maritimes.
Aug 2: First voyage Marseille-
Sydney.
1964 9,763 GRT.
1967 Feb 14: Arrived at Split to be
broken up by Brodospas.

Motorship *Zaandam*
Holland-America Line, Rotterdam

Builders: Wilton-Fijenoord,
Schiedam
Yard no: 663
10,909 GRT; 152.9 × 19.5 m /
502 × 64.0 ft; MAN diesels from
builders; Twin screw; 12,500 BHP;
17 kn; Passengers: 160 tourist
class.

1938 Aug 26: Floated in
construction dock. The name
originally intended had been
Schiedam.
Dec 21: Completed.
1939 Jan 7: Maiden voyage
Rotterdam-New York.
1940 Apr 27: First voyage New
York-Java.
1942 Taken over by US War
Shipping Administration as
transport.
Nov 2: While on a voyage from
Beira to New York the *Zaandam*
was torpedoed by the German
submarine *U 174* 300 nautical
miles north of Cape San Roque
and sank in position 01° 25′N-
36° 22′W. 135 dead. Three
survivors were found by a patrol
vessel, 82 days after the sinking.
Remarkably they had managed to
stay alive.

4

3/4 *The* Noordam *(3) and* Zaandam
*were used on the Rotterdam-New York
service.*

Motorship *Westerdam*
Holland-America Line, Rotterdam

Builders: Wilton-Fijenoord,
Schiedam
Yard no: 671
12,149 GRT; 157.9 × 20.1 m /
518 × 65.9 ft; MAN diesels from
builders; Twin screw; 10,400 BHP;
16 kn; Passengers: 134 1st class.

1940 Jul 27: Floated in
construction dock. Laid up,
incomplete.
Aug 27: The *Westerdam* was hit
during an Allied air-raid and sank.
Raised.
1944 Sep: Dutch resistance
fighters sank the *Westerdam* in
order to prevent the Germans from
using the hull as a blockship.
1945 Sep 13: Raised.
Repaired and completed at
Schiedam.
1946 Jun 28: Maiden voyage
Rotterdam-New York.
1965 Feb 3: Arrived at Alicante to
be broken up.

Motorship *Zuiderdam*
Holland-America Line, Rotterdam

Builders: Wilton-Fijenoord,
Schiedam
Yard no: 672
12,150 GRT; 157.9 × 20.1 m /
518 × 65.9 ft; MAN diesels from
builders: Twin screw; 10,400 BHP;
16 kn; Passengers: 134 1st class.

1941 Floated in construction
dock.
Aug 28: Burned out and capsized
after British air-raid.
1942 Jul 25: Raised and laid up at
Rotterdam.
1944 Sep 22: Sunk as blockship in
the Nieuwe Waterweg near
Maassluis.
1946 Nov 15: Raised.
1948 Apr: As the *Zuiderdam* was
not worth repairing, she was sold
to be broken up.
Jun 8: Towed from Rotterdam to
Ghent. Broken up by Van Heyghen
Frères.

5 *The last ship of the class, the*
Westerdam, *entered service in 1946.*
6 *The* Zuiderdam *was sunk as a block
ship during the Second World War
while still incomplete.*

Motorship *Wilhelm Gustloff*
Hamburg-South America Line,
Hamburg

Builders: Blohm & Voss, Hamburg
Yard no: 511
25,484 GRT; 208.5 × 23.6 m /
684 × 77.4 ft; MAN geared
diesels, B & V; Twin screw; 9,500
BHP; 15.5 kn; Passengers: 1,465
tourist class; Crew: 426.

1937 May 5: Launched.
1938 Mar 15: Completed.
The ship belonged to the German
Workers' Front and was managed
by Hamburg-South America for
cruises by the National Socialist
'Kraft durch Freude' (Strength
through Joy) association.
Apr 2: Maiden voyage, North Sea
cruising.
Apr 3: The *Wilhelm Gustloff*
received a distress call from the
British cargo vessel Pegaway,
which was in distress off
Terschelling.
Apr 4: Despite the stormy weather
the 19-man crew of the sinking
vessel was rescued.
Apr 10: Used as a floating 'polling
station' outside the three mile limit
for Germans resident in Britain
wishing to vote on Austrian
'Anschluss'. Collected passengers
at Tilbury and returned them the
same day.
1939 Sep 22: Commissioned as
hospital ship in the German Navy.
1940 Nov 20: Accommodation
ship at Gotenhafen (Gdynia).
1945 Jan 30: The *Wilhelm
Gustloff* left Gotenhafen with
6,100 people on board, mainly
refugees and wounded. At 21.06
hours, near Stolpmünde, the ship
was hit by three torpedoes from the
Soviet submarine *S-13* and began

to sink. The heavy cruiser *Admiral
Hipper,* which herself had 1,500
refugees on board, arrived on the
scene within a few minutes.
Because of the still-present
submarine danger the cruiser
broke off the rescue action which
had begun. At 22.18 hours the
Wilhelm Gustloff capsized and
sank 40 minutes later. The naval
units *Löwe, T 36, TF 19, TS 2,
M 341, V 1703* and the North
German Lloyd steamer *Göttingen,*
which had all been alerted by
radio, were able to rescue only 904
survivors from the icy water.

1/2 *The* Wilhelm Gustloff, *the first
new vessel for the KdF fleet, became a
hospital ship in 1939 (2).*

1

2

Diesel-electric vessel *Robert Ley*
Hamburg-America Line, Hamburg

Builders: Howaldt Hamburg
Yard no: 754
27,288 GRT; 203.8 × 24.0 m /
669 × 78.7 ft; MAN diesels, three
by MAN and three under licence
by builders, generators and electric
driving motors from Siemens-
Schuckertwerke; Twin screw;
8,800 SHP; 15 kn; Passengers:
1,774 tourist class; Crew: 435.

1938 Mar 29: Launched.
1939 Mar 24: Completed.
The ship belonged to the German
Workers' Front and was managed
by Hamburg-America Line for
cruises by the National Socialist
'Kraft durch Freude' (Strength
through Joy) assocation.
Apr 1: Maiden cruise.
Sep: Commissioned as naval
hospital ship at Gotenhafen
(Gdynia).
1940 Accommodation ship at
Gotenhafen.
1945 Used in the evacuation of the
German eastern territories.
Mar 24: The *Robert Ley* was hit
during an Allied air raid on
Hamburg and burned out.
1947 Jun 1: Towed to Great
Britain and broken up there.

3/4 *The slightly larger sister ship*
Robert Ley *was burned out at*
Hamburg shortly before the end of the
war and towed to England in 1947 to
be broken up (4).

Motorship *Boissevain*
Koninklijke Paketvaart Mij,
Batavia

Builders: Blohm & Voss, Hamburg
Yard no: 510
14,134 GRT; 170.5 × 22.0 m /
559 × 72.2 ft; Sulzer diesels;
Triple screw; 11,000 BHP; 16, max
18 kn; Passengers: 82 1st class, 82
2nd class, 500 steerage; Crew: 226.

1937 Jun 3: Launched.
Nov 2: Completed.
Dec 1: Delivered.
1938 Jan: First voyage. Used on
the route South Africa-
Netherlands Indies-Far East.
1940 Troop transport until 1946.
1947 Transferred to the new
Java-China Line, Amsterdam.
Kobe-South Africa-Buenos Aires
service.
1950 14,271 GRT.
1962 14,285 GRT.
1968 Jul 14: Arrived at Kaohsiung
to be broken up.

1 *The launching of the* Boissevain *in
June 1937.*
2/3 *Two pictures of the* Boissevain
undergoing trials.
4 *In 1947 the* Boissevain *and her two
sisterships were brought under the flag
of the newly-founded Java-China Line.*

1

Motorship *Tegelberg*
Koninklijke Paketvaart Mij,
Batavia

Builders: Nederlandsche SB Mij,
Amsterdam
Yard no: 243
14,150 GRT; 170.5 × 22.0 m /
559 × 72.2 ft; Sulzer diesels,
Werkspoor; Triple screw; 11,000
BHP; 16, max 18 kn; Passengers:
82 1st class, 82 2nd class, 500
steerage; Crew: 231.

1937 Jul 10: Launched.
1938 Mar 8: Completed.
Mar: First voyage in liner service
South Africa-Netherlands Indies-
Japan.
1942 Troop transport.
1946 Troop transport from
Indonesia.
1947 Transferred to the
newly-founded Java-China Line,
Amsterdam.
Liner service Kobe-South Africa-
Buenos Aires.
1950 14,281 GRT.
1963 14,300 GRT.
1968 Mar 14: Arrived at
Kaohsiung. Broken up there.

Motorship *Ruys*
Koninklijke Paketvaart Mij,
Batavia

Builders: 'De Schelde', Vlissingen
Yard no: 204
14,155 GRT; 170.5 × 22.0 m /
559 × 72.2 ft; Sulzer diesels, De
Schelde; Triple screw; 11,000
BHP; 16, max 18 kn; Passengers:
82 1st class, 82 2nd class; 500
steerage; Crew: 221.

1937 Sep 21: Launched.
1938 Mar 21: Trials.
Apr 7: Delivered.
South Africa-Netherlands Indies-
Japan service.
1940 Troop transport. Returned
to former old route after the war.
1947 Transferred to the newly
founded Java-China Line,
Amsterdam. Kobe-South Africa-
Buenos Aires service.
1950 14,285 GRT.
1962 14,304 GRT.
1968 Sep 13: Arrived at
Kaohsiung to be broken up.

5/6 *The Dutch-built sister ships to
the* Boissevain, *the* Tegelberg *(5) and
the* Ruys *(6).*

Circassia, Cilicia and Caledonia

Motorship *Circassia*
Anchor Line, Glasgow

Builders: Fairfield, Glasgow
Yard no: 661
11,137 GRT; 154.2 × 20.1 m /
506 × 65.9 ft; Doxford diesels,
Fairfield; Twin screw; 14,000
BHP; 16.5, max 18 kn;
Passengers: 321 1st class, 80
steerage.

1937 Jun 8: Launched.
Oct 19: Completed.
Oct 23: Maiden voyage Glasgow-
Liverpool-Bombay. Then
Liverpool-Bombay service.
1940 Jan: Commissioned as armed
merchant cruiser.
1942 Feb: Troop transport.
1943 Landing Ship Infantry
(Large).
1948 Liverpool-Bombay service
again after overhaul. 11,170 GRT.
1966 Apr 25: Arrived at Alicante.
Broken up there.

Motorship *Cilicia*
Anchor Line, Glasgow

1966 Jan Backx

Builders: Fairfield, Glasgow
Yard no: 664
11,137 GRT; 154.2 × 20.1 m /
506 × 65.9 ft; Doxford diesels,
Fairfield; Twin screw; 14,000
BHP; 16.5, max 18 kn;
Passengers: 320 1st class, 80
steerage.

1937 Oct 21: Launched.
1938 Jul: Completed.
Entered Liverpool-Bombay
service.
1939 Oct 15: Commissioned as
armed merchant cruiser.
1944 Mar: Refitted as troop
transport at Mobile, the work
lasting until December 16 1944.
1947 May 31: First post-war
voyage Liverpool-Bombay. 11,172
GRT.
1965 Nov: Sold to Stichting
Vakopleiding Havenbedrief,
Rotterdam.
1966 Refitted at the Verolme
shipyard as a stationary training
ship. Renamed *Jan Backx*.
Shipping school at Parkhaven.

Motorship *Caledonia*
Anchor Line, Glasgow

Builders: Fairfield, Glasgow
Yard no: 732
11,255 GRT; 154 × 20.2 m /
505 × 66.3 ft; Doxford diesels,
Fairfield; Twin screw; 14,000
BHP; 16.5, max 18 kn;
Passengers: 326 1st class, 80
steerage.

1947 Mar 12: Launched.
1948 Mar 23: Completed.
Liverpool-Bombay service.
1965 Sold to the Stichting voor
Studentenhuisvesting,
Amsterdam.
Dec 29: Arrived at Amsterdam, to
serve as an accommodation ship
for students.
1970 Mar: Taken to Hamburg
and broken up by the Ritscher firm
of Harburg.

1/2 The sister ships Cilicia *(1) and*
Circassia *(2) which were built for the
Liverpool-Bombay service. The*
Circassia *was the Anchor Line's first
motorship.*
3 A third ship in this class, the
Caledonia, *was built ten years later.*

3

The Oslofjord

Motorship *Oslofjord*
Norwegian America Line, Oslo

Builders: Deschimag AG 'Weser',
Bremen
Yard no: 932
18,673 GRT; 179.7 × 22.3 m /
590 × 73.2 ft; MAN geared
diesels, Weser; Twin screw; 17,600
BHP; 19.5 kn; Passengers: 152
cabin class, 307 tourist class, 401
3rd class; Crew: 310.

1937 Dec 29: Launched.
1938 May 10: Completed.
Jun 4: Maiden voyage Oslo-New
York.
1940 Laid up at New York during
the early part of the year.
Oct: Troop transport.
Dec 1: While on a voyage from
Liverpool to Newcastle the
Oslofjord struck a German
aircraft-laid mine off the mouth of
the Tyne. She sank in shallow
water off South Shields and broke
her back.

1

1/2 *After only two years of service the* Oslofjord *was sunk by a mine.*

Diesel-electric vessel *Patria*
Hamburg-America Line,
Hamburg

1945 *Empire Welland*
1946 *Rossia*

Builders: Deutsche Werft,
Hamburg
Yard no: 174
16,595 GRT; 182.2 × 22.5 m /
598 × 73.8 ft; MAN diesels, AEG
generators and driving motors;
Twin screw; 16,950 BHP; 17, max
18 kn; Passengers: 185 1st class,
164 tourist class; Crew: 241.

1938 Jan 15: Launched.
Jul 8: Delivered. While the *Patria*
was being docked subsequent to
trials, the floating-dock heeled
over because of a leak, the *Patria*

with it. The dock took a list of 30
degrees before touching the
bottom. However, the *Patria* was
recovered with minimal damage.
Jul 12: Cruise to the Northern
capitals.
Aug 27: Maiden voyage Hamburg-
South America-West Coast.
1940 Accommodation ship and
floating power station at Stettin.
1942 Naval accommodation ship
at Flensburg.
1945 May: The *Patria* became for
a short time the seat of the German
government.
Jul 1: Handed over to Great
Britain. Renamed *Empire
Welland*.
Refitted as a troop transport at
Belfast. 17,870 GRT. Two voyages
for the Ministry of Transport.

1946 Feb: Handed over to the
Soviet Union. Renamed *Rossia,*
with home port Odessa.
May: First voyage Liverpool-New
York.
1947 Feb 6: First voyage Batum-
New York, then Odessa-New
York service.
1948 Odessa-Batum service.

1 *The first large diesel-electric
passenger ship, the* Patria.
2 *The* Patria's *dock accident on July 8
1938.*
3 *The* Rossia *ex Patria.*

1

2

3

The Pasteur

Turbine steamer *Pasteur*
Cie Sudatlantique, Bordeaux

1959 *Bremen*
1972 *Regina Magna*

Builders: Penhoët, St Nazaire
Yard no: R 8
29,253 GRT; 212.4 × 26.8 m /
697 × 87.9 ft; Parsons geared
turbines, Penhoët; Quadruple
screw; 60,000 SHP; 23, max 25.5
kn; Passengers: 287 1st class, 126
2nd class, 338 3rd class; Crew:
540.

1938 Feb 15: Launched.
1939 Aug: Completed.
Sep 10: The ship's maiden voyage
Bordeaux-Buenos Aires, which
had been scheduled to start on this
day, was cancelled because of the
war.
1940 Jun 2: On her first voyage,
the *Pasteur* transported the French
gold reserves from Brest to
Halifax.
Aug: Entered service as a troop
transport under the British flag.
Managed by Cunard-White Star.
1945 Jun: Returned to the French
flag.
1946 Apr 11: Returned to the
French government. The ship
continued as a troop transport,
managed now by Cie
Sudatlantique.
1948 30,447 GRT.
1956 Jul: Laid up at Brest. The
Pasteur was given the 'Croix de
Guerre' for her services as a troop
transport.
1957 Sep 18: Sold to North
German Lloyd, Bremen.
1958 Jan: Rebuilt by Bremer
Vulkan, the work lasting until
1959. New boilers.
1959 Renamed *Bremen*. After
rebuilding, the ship measured
32,336 GRT. Passengers: 216 1st
class, 906 tourist class.
Jul 9: First voyage Bremerhaven-
New York. Also cruising.
1965/66 Refitted at the repair
yard of North German Lloyd.
Bulbous bow fitted. 32,360 GRT.
1970 Sep 1: Hamburg-America
and North German Lloyd Lines
amalgamated to form
Hapag-Lloyd AG.
1971 Oct: Sold to International
Cruises SA, Dimitri Chandris,
Piraeus, with delivery January
1972.
1972 Jan: Delivered to Chandris.
Renamed *Regina Magna*.
Cruising. Now measured at 23,801
GRT.
1974 Oct 17: Laid up at Piraeus.

1

1 *The* Pasteur *on her delivery voyage to Bremerhaven in 1957.*

2 *North German Lloyd had the* Pasteur *rebuilt as the* Bremen.

3 *In 1972 Chandris took over the* Regina Magna *ex* Bremen *ex* Pasteur.

Tanker San Jorge

Steamship *San Jorge*
Yacimientos Petroliferos Fiscales,
Buenos Aires

Builders: Blohm & Voss, Hamburg
Yard no: 516
10,006 GRT; 165.3 × 18.8 m /
542 × 61.7 ft; III exp engine,
Gutehoffnungshütte; Single screw;
7,000 IHP; 14, max 15 kn;
Passengers: 32 1st class, 28 3rd
class; Crew: 74.

1938 Mar 10: Launched.
Jun 28: Completed.
Jul 8: Delivered.
The *San Jorge* plies between the
Argentinian ports of Buenos Aires
and Comodoro Rivadavia.

1 *The launching of the* San Jorge.
2 *The* San Jorge *during trials. The
tanker has accommodation for 60
passengers.*

1

2

Turbine steamer *Canton*
P & O Line, London

Builders: Stephen, Glasgow
Yard no: 557
15,784 GRT; 171.5 × 22.3 m /
563 × 73.2 ft; Geared turbines,
Stephen; Twin screw; 18,500 SHP;
18, max 20 kn; Passengers: 260 1st
class, 220 2nd class; Crew: 370.

1938 Apr 14: Launched.
Sep 9: Completed.

Oct 7: Maiden voyage
Southampton-Hong Kong.
1939 Nov: Commissioned as an
armed merchant cruiser.
1944 Fitted out at Cape Town as
troop transport.
1946 Released from war service.
1947 Overhauled by Stephen at
Glasgow and refitted as a
passenger ship. 16,033
GRT. Passengers: 298 1st class,
244 tourist class.

Oct: First post-war voyage
Southampton-Hong Kong.
1962 Aug 31: From London to
Hong Kong. Broken up there by
Leung Yau Shipbreaking Co.

1/2 The Canton *entered service in
1938, the last P & O passenger liner to
have a black hull. When she was
overhauled in 1947 after her war
service, the hull was painted white.*

1

2

The Two Stockholms

Motorship *Stockholm*
Swedish-America Line,
Gothenburg

Builders: CR dell'Adriatico,
Monfalcone
28,000 GRT; 205.6 × 25.4 m /
675 × 63.3 ft; Sulzer diesels from
builders; Triple screw; 20,000
BHP; 19 kn; Passengers: 1,350 in
cabin, tourist and 3rd class; 640
passengers in one class while
cruising.

1938 May 29: Launched.
Dec 19/20: The nearly-completed
ship was completely burned out as
the result of an electrical short
circuit, and had to be scrapped. In
accordance with the contract she
was to have been handed over to
the Line on March 1 1939.

1/2 *The launching of the* Stockholm
*in May 1938. In December of the same
year the almost complete ship was
totally destroyed by fire.*

1

2

Motorship *Stockholm*
Swedish-America Line,
Gothenburg

1941 *Sabaudia*

Builders: CR dell'Adriatico,
Monfalcone
Yard no: 1203
29,307 GRT; 205.6 × 25.4 m /
675 × 83.3 ft; Sulzer diesels from
builders; Triple screw; 20,000
BHP; 19 kn; Passengers: 1,350 in
cabin, tourist and 3rd class; 640
passengers in one class while
cruising.

1939 Jan: After the *Stockholm* of
1938 had been destroyed by fire
shortly before completion, the
shipping company ordered an
identical replacement, which was
to be delivered at the beginning of
1941. The second *Stockholm*
received her predecessor's engines,
along with various other pieces of
equipment which were awaiting
fitting at the time of the fire.
1940 Mar 10: Launched.
1941 Oct: Completed.
Nov: As the war progressed, the
owners could find no immediate
use for their ship so she was taken
over by the Italian government and
management was given to 'Italia'
SAN. Renamed *Sabaudia*.
1942 Troop transport. Later, laid
up at Trieste.
1943 Sep 9: German
accommodation ship at Trieste
following the Italian capitulation.
1944 Jul 6: The *Sabaudia* was hit
during a British air raid on Trieste,
caught fire and sank.
1949 The wreck was raised and
scrapped.

3/4 *Swedish-America Line ordered a
second* Stockholm *as a replacement for
the one destroyed by fire. She was
launched in March 1940. However,
this ship too was never delivered to the
company which ordered it, but
commissioned instead on completion
as an Italian troop transport.*

5 *The wreck of the* Sabaudia *ex*
Stockholm.

4

The Dominion Monarch

Motorship *Dominion Monarch*
Shaw, Savill & Albion,
Southampton

1962 *Dominion Monarch Maru*

Builders: Swan, Hunter &
Wigham Richardson, Newcastle
Yard no: 1547
27,155 GRT; 207.8 × 25.8 m /
682 × 84.6 ft; Doxford diesels,
two of the four diesels from
builders; Quadruple screw; 32,000
BHP; 19.5, max 21.5 kn;
Passengers: 517 1st class; Crew:
385.

1938 Jul 27: Launched.
1939 Jan: Completed.
Feb 17: Maiden voyage
Southampton-Wellington.
1940 Aug: In service as troop
transport.
1947 Jul: Refitted as a passenger
ship, the work lasting until 1948.
26,463 GRT. 508 1st class
passengers.
1948 Entered London-Wellington
service at end of year.
1962 Jun: The *Dominion
Monarch* was stationed at Seattle,
where she served until November
as a floating hotel for visitors to the
World's Fair.
Nov 25: The liner arrived at
Osaka, where she was broken up
by Mitsui. She had been renamed
Dominion Monarch Maru for the
voyage Seattle-Osaka.

1 *The largest Shaw, Savill & Albion
passenger ship was the* Dominion
Monarch.

Turbine steamer *Mauretania*
Cunard-White Star Line,
Liverpool

Builders: Cammell Laird,
Birkenhead
Yard no: 1029
35,738 GRT; 235.4 × 27.3 m /
772 × 89.6 ft; Parsons geared
turbines from builders: Twin
screw; 42,000 SHP; 23 kn;
Passengers: 440 cabin class, 450
tourist class, 470 3rd class; Crew:
780.

1938 Jul 28: Launched.

1939 May 31: Completed.
Jun 17: Maiden voyage Liverpool-
New York.
Aug: First voyage Southampton-
New York.
Dec: Laid up at New York.
1940 Mar 6: Troop transport.
Transferred to Sydney and refitted
there, the work being completed in
May.
1946 Sep 2: Released from war
service. Overhauled by Cammell
Laird at Liverpool.
1947 Apr 26: First post-war
voyage Liverpool-New York.

Jun 10: Service Southampton-New
York.
Now 35,677 GRT. 475 1st class,
390 cabin class, 300 tourist class.
1958 35,655 GRT.
1962 Dec: The *Mauretania* was
painted bright green and used
thenceforward mainly for cruising.
1965 Nov 23: Arrival at
Inverkeithing, where she was
broken up by T.W. Ward.

1/2 *The* Mauretania *in 1954 (1), and
as a cruise liner with a green hull in
1963 (2).*

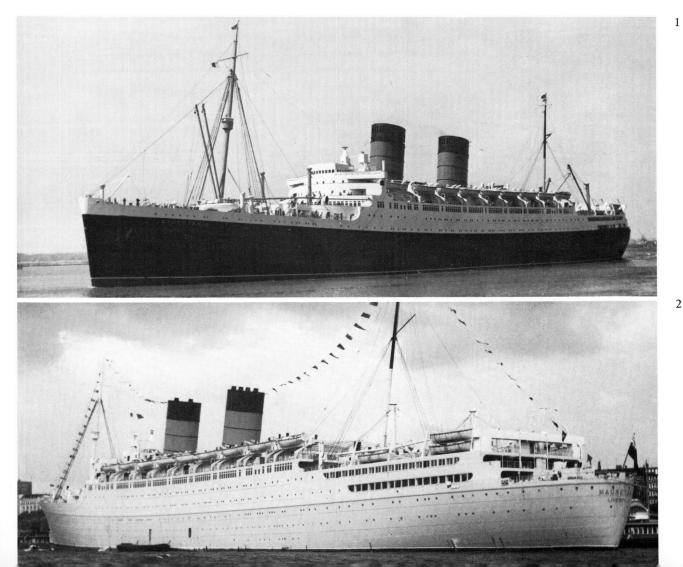

1

2

The Tjitjalengka

Motorship *Tjitjalengka*
Java-China-Java Line, Batavia

Builders: Nederlandsche SB Mij,
Amsterdam
Yard no: 271
10,972 GRT; 145.1 × 19.7 m /
476 × 64.6 ft; Stork diesels; Single
screw; 6,000 BHP; 15 kn;
Passengers: 64 1st class, 55 2nd
class, 100 3rd class, 1,129 on deck;
Crew: 162.

1938 Aug 16: Launched.
1939 Apr 29: Completed.
May: Liner service Netherlands
Indies-Far East.
1940 Troop transport.
1942 Jul 8: Chartered to the
British Admiralty. Fitted out as
hospital ship.
1946 Feb: Returned to her
owners.
During the war and until 1947,
registered at Willemstad.
1947 Transferred to Java-China
Line, Amsterdam, formed through
amalgamation with KPM. Entered
the Kobe-South Africa-Buenos
Aires service.
1959 Sep 27: During a typhoon
the *Tjitjalengka* was driven ashore
near Nagoya and was not refloated
until three months later, on
December 16.
1968 May 11: Arrival at Hong
Kong, where she was broken up by
Ming Hing & Co.

1/2 The Dutch passenger ship
Tjitjalengka, *which was completed in
May 1939, served as a hospital ship
during the Second World War.*

Motorship *Sobieski*
Gdynia-America Line, Gdynia

1950 *Gruzia*

Builders: Swan, Hunter &
Wigham Richardson, Newcastle
Yard no: 1572
11,030 GRT; 156.1 × 20.4 m /
512 × 66.9 ft; Burmeister & Wain
diesels, Kincaid; Twin screw;
8,700 BHP; 16, max 17 kn;
Passengers: 44 1st class, 250 3rd
class, 860 steerage; Crew: 260.

1938 Aug 25: Launched.
1939 May: Completed.
Jun 15: Maiden voyage Gdynia-
South America.
Sep: At the outbreak of war the
Sobieski was at Dakar.
Oct: Transferred to Great Britain
and refitted as a troop transport.
1947 Handed back to Gdynia-
America Line. Passengers: 70 1st
class, 270 cabin class, 600 tourist
class.
May 14: First voyage Genoa-New
York.
1950 Sold to the Soviet Union.

Renamed *Gruzia*. Home port
Odessa. Used in the Black Sea on
the Odessa-Batum route.
1975 Apr 14: Arrived at La Spezia
to be broken up.

Motorship *Chrobry*
Gdynia-America Line, Gdynia

Builders: Nakskov Skibsvaerft
11,442 GRT; 154.2 × 20.3 m /
506 × 66.6 ft; Burmeister & Wain
diesels; Twin screw; 8,700 BHP;
16, max 18.43 kn; Passengers: 60
1st class, 303 3rd class, 804
steerage; Crew: 260.

1939 Feb 25: Launched.
Jul: Completed.
Jul 27: Maiden voyage
Gdynia-South America.
Sep: At the outbreak of war the
Chrobry was in Brazil.
Oct: The ship arrived in Great
Britain and was fitted out as a
troop transport.
1940 May 14: While bound for
Norway carrying troops, the
Chrobry was attacked by German
aircraft off Bodö and caught fire.
12 of the crew and an unknown
number of troops lost their lives.
May 15: The completely burnt-out
Chrobry sank in position 67° 40′N-
13° 50′E.

1

2

3

1/2 *The* Sobieski *was taken over by Great Britain following the collapse of Poland, and used as a troop transport (1). Picture 2 shows the* Gruzia *ex* Sobieski *in the Kiel canal.*

3 *The* Sobieski's *sister ship, the Danish-built* Chrobry, *was sunk by German bombers in 1940.*

Nederland Liner Oranje

Motorship *Oranje*
Stoomvaart Mij 'Nederland',
Amsterdam

1964 *Angelina Lauro*

Builders: Nederlandsche SB Mij,
Amsterdam
Yard no: 270
20,017 GRT; 199.9 × 25.5 m /
656 × 83.7 ft; Sulzer diesels;
37,500 BHP; Twin screw; 21, max
26.5 kn; Passengers: 665 in 1st,
2nd and 3rd class, 52 4th class.

1938 Sep 8: Launched.
1939 Jun 27: Completed.
Aug 4: Cruising
Amsterdam-Madeira.
Sep 4: Maiden voyage Amsterdam-
Batavia.
Dec: Laid up at Sourabaya.
1941 Feb: Transferred to Sydney
and there fitted out as a hospital
ship.
Jul 30: Entered service as a
hospital ship in the Royal
Australian Navy. The *Oranje*
remained however under the
Dutch flag.
1946 Jul 19: Handed back to
'Nederland'. Re-entered
Amsterdam-Batavia service.
1950 Feb: First voyage
Amsterdam-Panama-Auckland-
Sydney-Singapore-Suez-
Amsterdam.
1959 Jan 13: Refitted at
Amsterdam. 20,551 GRT.
Passengers: 323 1st class, 626
tourist class.
1964 Sep 4: Sold to Achille Lauro,
Rome. Renamed *Angelina Lauro*.
Extensively rebuilt by Cant del
Tirreno, Genoa, the work lasting
until 1966.
1965 Aug 24/26: Six people lost
their lives in a large fire during the
rebuilding work.
1966 With the completion of
work: 24,377 GRT; 205.5 m /
674 ft length overall; Passengers:
189 1st class, 377 alternatively 1st
or tourist class, 1,050 tourist class.
Mar 6: First voyage Bremerhaven-
Wellington.
1968 First voyage Southampton-
Sydney.
1972 Cruising only.

1/2 *Picture 1 shows the original
external appearance of the 'Nederland'
liner* Oranje, *which is depicted in
picture 2 as a hospital ship in the Royal
Australian Navy.*
3/4 *The* Oranje *after the 1959 refit* (3)
and as the Angelina Lauro *in 1967* (4).

1

2

3

4

Panama Railroad Liners

Turbine steamer *Panama*
Panama Railroad, New York

1941 *James Parker*
1946 *Panama*
1957 *President Hoover*
1964 *Regina*
1973 *Regina Prima*

Builders: Bethlehem Steel Co,
Quincy
Yard no: 1467
10,021 GRT; 150.3 × 19.5 m /
493 × 64.0 ft; Geared turbines
from builders; Twin screw; 9,150
SHP; 17, max 18.5 kn; Passengers:
202 1st class.

1938 Launched.
1939 Apr: Completed.
New York-Cristobal service.
1941 Jun 13:Taken over as US
Army transport *James Parker.*
Refitted by Atlantic Basin Iron
Works at New York.
1946 Jan: Handed over to US
Maritime Commission.
May 15: Renamed *Panama* after
refit as passenger ship.
New York-Cristobal service again
for Panama Railroad.
1948 9,978 GRT.
1953 Owning company changed
its name to Panama Canal Co,
New York.
1957 Jan 12: Sold to American
President Lines, San Francisco.
Renamed *President Hoover.*
10,603 GRT.
San Francisco-Hong Kong service.
1964 Dec 2: To Dimitri Chandris,
Piraeus. Registered for
International Cruises, SA.
1965 Refitted at Piraeus. 650
passengers in one class.
Mediterranean cruising.
Caribbean cruising during the
winter.
1967 10,153 GRT. Registered for

International Cruises SA,
Panama.
1973 Renamed *Regina Prima*.

1/2 *The* Panama *in 1941 (1) and at Venice in 1966 as a Chandris Cruise liner (2).*

2

Turbine steamer *Ancon*
Panama Railroad, New York

1963 *State of Maine*

Builders: Bethlehem Steel Co,
Quincy
Yard no: 1468
10,021 GRT; 150.3 × 19.5 m /
493 × 64.0 ft; Geared turbines
from builders; Twin screw; 9,150
SHP; 17, max 18.66 kn;
Passengers: 202 1st class.

1938 Sep 24: Launched.
1939 Placed in New York-
Cristobal service after completion.
1942 Jan 11: Commissioned as
transport by the US Army.
Aug 7: To US Navy.
1946 Feb 25: Handed over to US
Maritime Commission. Re-entered
New York-Cristobal service for
Panama Railroad.
1948 9,978 GRT.
1953 The company changed its
name to Panama Canal Co.
1961 Jun: Laid up and offered for
sale.
1962 Jun 29: Sold to US
Department of Commerce, New
York. Renamed *State of Maine*
and fitted out as a training ship.
1963 Commissioned as a training
ship by Maine Maritime Academy.
1973 May 9: Sold to the North
American Smelting Co,
Wilmington, to be broken up.

Turbine steamer *Cristobal*
Panama Railroad, New York

Builders: Bethlehem Steel Co,
Quincy
Yard no: 1469
10,021 GRT; 150.3 × 19.5 m /
493 × 64.0 ft; Geared turbines
from builders; Twin screw; 9,150
SHP; 17, max 18.66 kn;
Passengers: 202 1st class.

1939 Mar 4: Launched.
Aug: Completed.
Aug 17: Maiden voyage New York-
Cristobal.
1942 Jan: Commissioned as a
transport by the US Army.
1946 Jun 14: Handed back to
Panama Railroad.
1948 9,978 GRT.
1953 Owning company's name
now Panama Canal Co.
1962 Home port New Orleans.

3 *The* State of Maine *ex* Ancon *at
Rotterdam in June 1970.*
4 *The* Cristobal, *the third ship of the
class.*

The Queen Elizabeth

Turbine steamer *Queen Elizabeth*
Cunard-White Star Line,
Liverpool

1969 *Elizabeth*
1970 *Seawise University*

Builders: Brown, Clydebank
Yard no: 552
83,673 GRT; 313.5 × 36.1 m /
1,029 × 118.4 ft; Parsons geared
turbines, Brown; Quadruple
screw; 200,000 SHP; 28.5, max 32
kn; Passengers: 823 1st class; 662
cabin class, 798 tourist class;
Crew: 1,296.

1938 Sep 27: Launched.
1940 Feb 27: Largely completed,
the *Queen Elizabeth* left the
shipyard for transfer to New York
because of the threat of attack
from the Luftwaffe. To confuse
agents and spies, the story was
circulated that this was to be a
positioning voyage to
Southampton. The ship left the
Clyde on March 2 without having
undergone any trials (only the
compass had been adjusted) and
reached New York without
incident on March 7. The liner was
laid up next to the *Mauretania,
Queen Mary* and *Normandie.*
Nov: The *Queen Elizabeth* was
needed as a troop transport. She
sailed via Singapore, where she
docked, to Sydney, and was there
fitted out as a troop transport.
1946 Mar 6: The *Queen Elizabeth*
was the first Cunard liner to be
released from war service. She was
refitted as a passenger ship at
Southampton and Gourock.
Oct 16: Maiden voyage
Southampton-New York.
1965 Dec 5: Arrived at Greenock
for general overhaul, thereafter
82,998 GRT.
1968 The *Queen Elizabeth* sailed
out of Southampton for the last
time. On December 8 the ship
arrived at Port Everglades, where
it had been planned to use her as a
convention centre and tourist
attraction. Cunard had a
controlling interest in the
Elizabeth Corporation which had
been founded for this purpose.
1969 Jul 19: The ship was sold to
Queen Ltd, Port Everglades.
Renamed *Elizabeth.* This
company also intended to use the
ship as a convention centre.
1970 Aug: Bankruptcy of Queen
Ltd. The Chinese shipowner
C.Y. Tung bought the *Elizabeth* at
an auction. The ship was
registered at Hong Kong in the
name of Seawise Foundations Ltd.
Renamed *Seawise University.*
1971 Feb 10: The *Seawise
University* left Port Everglades for
Hong Kong where she arrived on
July 16. The voyage had been held
up several times by boiler trouble.
Work was begun at Hong Kong on
a thorough overhaul of the ship
which C.Y. Tung wished to put
into service as a floating university
and cruise liner.
1972 Jan 9: During the refitting
fire broke out which spread to the
whole ship.
Jan 10: The ship heeled over. It
was not until January 13, with half
of the ship's breadth protruding
from the water, that the fire died
down.
1974 Work begun on removal of
wreck.

1

1/2 *The* Queen Elizabeth, *the largest passenger ship ever built.*
3 *In January 1972 the* Seawise University *ex* Queen Elizabeth *was completely burnt out and sank.*

Motorship *Argentina Maru*
Osaka Shosen KK, Osaka

1943 *Kaiyo*

Builders: Mitsubishi, Nagasaki
Yard no: 734
12,755 GRT; 167.3 × 20.9 m /
549 × 68.6 ft; Sulzer diesels from
builders; Twin screw; 16,500 BHP;
21.5 kn; Passengers: 101 1st class,
130 3rd class, 670 3rd class in
dormitories.

1938 Dec 9: Launched.
1939 Jul: Completed.
Entered Japan-South America
service.
1941 Dec: Troop transport.
1942 Dec: Converted to aircraft
carrier by Mitsubishi, work lasting
until 1943. The ship was fitted with
turbine machinery of 52,000 SHP
for 24 knots.
1943 Nov 23: Commissioned as
aircraft carrier *Kaiyo*.
1945 Jul 24: The *Kaiyo* was
attacked and sunk by US aircraft
in Beppu Bay, 10 nautical miles
northwest of Oita.
The wreck was broken up at
Beppu.

Motorship *Brazil Maru*
Osaka Shosen KK, Osaka

Builders: Mitsubishi, Nagasaki
Yard no: 735
12,733 GRT; 167.3 × 20.9 m /
549 × 68.6 ft; Sulzer diesels from
builders; Twin screw; 16,500 SHP;
21.5 kn; Passengers: 101 1st class,
130 3rd class, 670 3rd class in
dormitories.

1939 Aug 2: Launched.
Dec 23: Delivered.
Entered Japan-South America
service on completion.
1941 Dec: Troop transport.
1942 Conversion to aircraft carrier
planned, like her sister ship
Argentina Maru.
Aug 5: The *Brazil Maru* was
torpedoed by the US submarine
Greenling northwest of Truk and
sank in position 09° 51′N-
150° 46′E.

1

2

1/2 In 1939 Osaka Shosen KK placed the sister ships Argentina Maru *and* Brazil Maru *in their Japan-South America service. Both ships were converted to aircraft carriers during the Second World War and later lost.*

Motorship *Hokoku Maru*
Osaka Shosen KK, Osaka

Builders: Tama SB Co
10,438 GRT; 163.8 × 20.2 m /
537 × 66.3 ft; Burmeister & Wain
diesels, Mitsubishi; Twin screw;
13,000 BHP; 17, max 21 kn;
Passengers: 48 1st class, 48 3rd
class, 304 3rd class in dormitories.

1939 Jul 5: Launched.
1940 Completed.
Japan-Europe service.
1941 Aug: Refit commenced as
auxiliary cruiser.
1942 Mar 10: Commissioned by
Japanese Navy.
Nov 11:The *Hokoku Maru* was
operating in the Indian Ocean with
her sister ship *Aikoku Maru,*
which also had been fitted out as
an auxiliary cruiser. The two ships
intercepted the 6,341 GRT Dutch
tanker *Ondina,* being escorted by
the Indian frigate *Bengal* (733
tons) in position 19° 45′S-
92°40′E. The Japanese opened fire
at close range on the hopelessly
inferior convoy. However, their
intended victims returned fire most
effectively, and because the
distance involved was only about
1,200 yards they scored some
direct hits which led to explosions
on the *Hokoku Maru.* The badly
damaged *Ondina* was abandoned
by her crew. The *Bengal* was also
considerably damaged. On the
Japanese side, the *Hokoku Maru*
sank, while the damaged *Aikoku
Maru* ceased fire in the belief that
both of the enemy ships had been
sunk.
In the meantime, the crew of the
Ondina reboarded the tanker and
made course for Fremantle,
assuming that their escort frigate

had been sunk.
The badly damaged *Bengal* sailed
to Colombo.

Motorship *Aikoku Maru*
Osaka Shosen KK, Osaka

Builders: Tama SB Co
Yard no: 760
10,437 GRT; 163.8 × 20.2 m /
537 × 66.3 ft; Burmeister & Wain
diesels, Mitsubishi; Twin screw;
13,000 BHP; 17, max 21 kn;
Passengers: 48 1st class, 48 3rd
class, 304 3rd class dormitories.

1939 Launched.
1940 Completed.
Japan-Europe service.
1941 Aug: Refit commenced as
auxiliary cruiser.
1942 Mar 10: Commissioned by
the Japanese Navy.
1943 Oct 1: Entered service as
transport.
1944 Feb 17: The *Aikoku Maru*
was attacked by US aircraft near
Truk Atoll and sank in position
07° 22′N-151° 54′E.

Motorship *Gokoku Maru*
Osaka Shosen KK, Osaka

Builders: Tama SB Co
10,438 GRT; 163.8 × 20.2 m /
537 × 66.3 ft; Burmeister & Wain
diesels, Mitsubishi; Twin screw;
13,000 BHP; 17, max 21 kn;
Passengers: 48 1st class, 48 3rd
class, 304 3rd class dormitories.

1941 Launched.
The ship was not completed as a
passenger vessel, but fitted out as
an auxiliary cruiser.
1942 Sep 25: Commissioned by
the Japanese Navy.
Dec 18: The *Gokoku Maru* was
badly damaged at Madang by US
aircraft.
1943 Oct 1: Entered service as
transport.
Dec 27: Badly damaged by a mine
off Omae Zaki.
1944 Oct 10: The *Gokoku Maru*
was torpedoed and sunk by the US
submarine *Barb* northwest of
Hiroshima in position 32° 31′N-
129° 10′E.

3 *The three sister ships ordered for the European service,* Hokoku Maru *(3),* Aikoku Maru *and* Gokoku Maru *also fell victim to the Second World War.*

The Baudouinville

Motorship *Baudouinville*
Compagnie Maritime Belge,
Antwerp

1942 *Lindau*

Builders: Cockerill, Hoboken
Yard no: 675
13,761 GRT; 165.1 × 20.6 m /
542 × 67.6 ft; Burmeister & Wain
diesels, Cockerill; Twin screw;
9,000 BHP; 17 kn; Passengers: 179
1st class, 216 2nd class; Crew: 255.

1939 May 18: Floated in Cockerill
construction dock.
May 21: First trials.
Jun 14: The ship was christened by
Prince Baudouin of Belgium.
Jul 7: Maiden voyage Antwerp-
Belgian Congo.
After three round voyages, because
of the war the ship was laid up at
Antwerp.
1940 May 10: Shortly before the
entry of German troops the
Baudouinville sailed for St
Nazaire to avoid capture.
Jun: Seized at Bordeaux by the
German Navy.
1941 Oct 20: The management of
the ship was made over to German
Africa Lines, Hamburg.
Oct 28: Commissioned as hospital
ship *Lindau*. 959 beds.
1943 Jan 1: Released from
hospital service. Used as an
accommodation ship.
1944 Aug 10: During the
evacuation of Nantes the *Lindau*
was set on fire by the Germans,
and sank after being severely
damaged by an explosion amongst
ammunition which had been
stored on board.
1946 Raised.
Aug 29: Arrived at Antwerp to be
broken up.

1947 Oct 21: The hull was towed
to Boom and there broken up.

1 *CMB's* Baudouinville *entered service
in July 1939.*
2 *In 1940 the Germans seized the ship,
setting fire to her as they retreated
from Nantes in 1944.*

1

2

Royal Mail Liner Andes

Turbine steamer *Andes*
Royal Mail Lines, London

Builders: Harland & Wolff,
Belfast
Yard no: 1005
25,689 GRT; 204.0 × 25.4 m /
669 × 83.3 ft; Geared turbines,
H & W; Twin screw; 30,000 SHP;
21 kn; Passengers: 403 1st class,
204 2nd class; Crew: 451.

1939 Mar 7:Launched.
On the outbreak of war the ship
was taken over for conversion to a
troop transport. She was to have
sailed on her maiden voyage to
South America on September 26.
Dec 9: First voyage as a troop
transport, to Halifax.
1945 May: The *Andes* carried the
Norwegian government-in-exile
back to Oslo.

1947 Released from war service.
Refitted for passenger service by
Harland & Wolff at Belfast.
25,676 GRT. Passengers: 324 1st
class, 204 2nd class.
1948 Jan 22: First voyage
Southampton-La Plata.
1959 Nov: Rebuilt as cruise liner
by 'De Schelde' at Vlissingen, the
work lasting until May 1960. 480
passengers in one class. White
hull. 25,895 GRT.
1960 Jun 10: First cruise after
refit.
1971 May 7: Arrived at Ghent to
be broken up by van Heyghen
Frères.

*1/3 Built in 1939 for the La Plata
service, the* Andes *was rebuilt as a
cruise liner in 1959. Picture 3 shows
her at the breakers' yard in 1971.*

1

2

3

Motorship *Klipfontein*
United Netherlands Navigation
Co, The Hague

Builders: Smit jr, Rotterdam
Yard no: 517
10,544 GRT; 158.5 × 19.2 m /
520 × 63.0 ft; Burmeister & Wain
diesels, Smit; Twin screw; 11,800
BHP; 17, max 20.5 kn;
Passengers: 106 1st class, 42
tourist class; Crew: 120.

1939 Mar 4: Launched.
Jul 11: Completed. Europe-
Lourenço Marques service.
1942 The *Klipfontein* became
transport for the US War Shipping
Administration.
1946 Feb 1: Returned to owners.
1953 Jan 8: During a voyage from
Lourenço Marques to Beira, the
Klipfontein struck some
submerged rocks near Inhambane,
five nautical miles off Cape Barra.
The forward bunker exploded. The
ship was abandoned, and sank
after 45 minutes. The passengers
and crew were picked up by the
Union-Castle liner *Bloemfontein
Castle*.

Motorship *Oranjefontein*
United Netherlands Navigation
Co, The Hague

1967 *Fontein*

Builders: Smit jr, Rotterdam
Yard no: 532
10,544 GRT; 160.6 × 19.1 m /
527 × 62.7 ft; Burmeister & Wain
diesels, Smit; Twin screw; 11,800
BHP; 17, max 20.5 kn;
Passengers: 100 1st class, 60
tourist class; Crew: 110.

1940 Mar 21: Launched.
Dec 20: Completed.
1941 Mar 17: Seized by the
German Navy.
Aug 28: Damaged by bombs at
Rotterdam. The management of
the *Oranjefontein* was made over
to German Africa Lines,
Hamburg, and the ship used for
target practice by the Luftwaffe
and U-boats.
1945 Refugee transport in the
evacuation of the German eastern
territories. (It has been stated, but
not officially confirmed, that the
ship was renamed *Pionier* in 1945.)
Jul 12: The *Oranjefontein* was
returned to VNSM.
Sep 12: The liner sailed from
Newcastle, where she had been
overhauled, to the Netherlands
Indies to repatriate Dutch citizens.
Afterwards, the *Oranjefontein*
made her first voyage in the
Europe-Africa service for which
she had been built.
1967 Aug: Sold to be broken up in
Spain. Renamed *Fontein* for the
handing-over voyage.
Aug 11: Arrived at Bilbao.

1 *The first of three sister ships, the*
Klipfontein *entered service in 1939.*
2 *The* Oranjefontein *was seized by the
Germans immediately on completion,
and did not sail on her first voyage to
Africa until 1945.*

Motorship *Jagersfontein*
United Netherlands Navigation
Co, The Hague

Launched as *Elandsfontein*
1967 *Devon*

Builders: Schichau, Danzig
10,574 GRT; 160.9 × 19.1 m /
528 × 62.7 ft; Sulzer diesels; Twin
screw; 11,800 BHP; 17, max 20 kn;
Passengers: 100 1st class, 60
tourist class; Crew: 110.

1939 Laid down as *Rietfontein*.
This was changed to *Elandsfontein*
before launching.
1940 Mar 30: Launched.
During the war the *Elandsfontein*
was taken over by the German
Navy, but was not completed for
service.
1945 Mar 14: During the fighting
around Gotehafen (Gdynia), the
ship was badly damaged by
artillery fire and sank in the mouth
of the Vistula.
1947 Mar 20: Raised.
Aug 9: Temporarily patched up for
the voyage, the wreck was towed to
Vlissingen, for completion at the
'De Schelde' yard.
1948 Renamed *Jagersfontein*.
1950 Mar 11: Completed. Entered
service on the Hamburg-Durban-
Lourenço Marques route.
1967 Nov: Sold to Embajada Cia
Naviera SA, Piraeus. Renamed
Devon. Sold immediately
afterwards to be broken up.
Dec 23: Arrived at Kaohsiung.

3/4 The *Jagersfontein* *was launched in*
1940 under the name Elandsfontein.
Picture 3 shows the ship being towed to
Holland in 1947.

New Ships for Nippon Yusen KK

Turbine steamer *Nitta Maru*
Nippon Yusen KK, Tokyo

1942 Chuyo

Builders: Mitsubishi, Nagasaki
Yard no: 750
17,150 GRT; 179.8 × 22.5 m /
590 × 73.8 ft; Zoelly geared
turbines; Twin screw; 25,200 SHP;
21, max 22.5 kn; Passengers: 115
1st class, 100 2nd class, 70 3rd
class.

1939 May 20: Launched.
1940 Mar 23: Delivered.
Intended for Yokohama-Hamburg
service, the *Nitta Maru* entered
service on the Yokohama-San
Francisco route because of the war
in Europe.
1942 May 1: The *Nitta Maru*
arrived at the shipyard at Kure for
conversion to an aircraft carrier.
Nov 25: The escort aircraft carrier
Chuyo was commissioned by the
Japanese Navy.
1943 Dec 4: The *Chuyo* was
torpedoed by the US submarine
Sailfish 260 nautical miles
southwest of Yokosuka and sank
in position 32° 37′N-143° 39′E.

Turbine steamer *Yawata Maru*
Nippon Yusen KK, Tokyo

1942 Unyo

Builders: Mitsubishi, Nagasaki
Yard no: 751
17,128 GRT; 179.8 × 22.5 m /
590 × 73.8 ft; Zoelly geared
turbines; Twin screw; 25,200 SHP;
21, max 22.16 kn; Passengers: 115
1st class, 100 2nd class, 70 3rd
class.

1939 Oct 31: Launched.

1940 Jul 31: Delivered.
Intended for the
Yokohama-Hamburg service, the
Yawata Maru entered the
trans-Pacific service Yokohama-
San Francisco because of the
outbreak of war in Europe.
1942 Jan: The *Yawata Maru*
arrived at Kure for conversion to
an aircraft carrier.
May 31: Commissioned by the
Japanese Navy as the escort aircraft
carrier *Unyo*.
1944 Sep 16: The *Unyo* was
torpedoed by the American
submarine *Barb* 220 nautical miles
southeast of Hong Kong and sank
in position 19° 18′N-116°26′E.

Turbine steamer *Kasuga Maru*
Nippon Yusen KK, Tokyo

1941 Taiyo

Builders: Mitsubishi, Nagasaki
Yard no: 752
17,127 GRT; 179.8 × 22.5 m /
590 × 73.8 ft; Zoelly geared
turbines, Mitsubishi; Twin screw;
25,200 SHP; 21 kn; Passengers:
115 1st class, 100 2nd class, 70 3rd
class.

1940 Sep 19: Launched.
Intended for the Yokohama-
Hamburg service, the *Kasuga
Maru* was never completed as a
passenger ship. In November 1940
the Japanese Navy took over the
ship's hull, and had it completed
as an aircraft carrier by Mitsubishi
under yard number 888.
1941 Sep 5: Delivery of the carrier
Taiyo.
Sep 15: Commissioned by the
Japanese Navy.

1944 Aug 18: The *Taiyo* was
torpedoed by the US submarine
Rasher 22 nautical miles southwest
of Cape Bojeador and sank in
position 18° 16′N-120° 20′E.

Motorship *Miike Maru*
Nippon Yusen KK, Tokyo

Builders: Mitsubishi, Nagasaki
Yard no: 760
11,739 GRT; 163.0 × 20.0 m /
535 × 65.6 ft; diesels, Mitsubishi;
Twin screw; 14,000 BHP; 20, max
20.6 kn; Passengers: 100 tourist
class, 136 3rd class.

1941 Apr 12: Launched.
Sep 30: Delivered.
Intended for the Kobe-Vancouver-
Seattle service. Immediately on
completion she was fitted out as a
troop transport at Ujina and
placed in service.
1944 Apr 21: The *Miike Maru* was
torpedoed by the American
submarine *Trigger* near the
Caroline Islands, southwest of
Yap, and sank in position
08° 34′N-134° 48′E. 18 dead.

1 *The* Nitta Maru *entered service in
1940, the first of a trio intended for the
Yokohama-Hamburg service. Because
of the war she sailed on the trans-
Pacific route.*
2/3 *The* Yawata Maru *(2) was
converted to an aircraft carrier, as was
her sister-ship* Kasuga Maru. *Picture 3
shows the* Taiyo ex Kasuga Maru.

1

2

3

Motorship *Aki Maru*
Nippon Yusen KK, Tokyo

Builders: Mitsubishi, Nagasaki
Yard no: 761
11,409 GRT; 163 × 20.0 m /
535 × 65.6 ft; diesels, Mitsubishi;
Twin screw; 14,000 BHP; 20 kn;
Passengers: 137 1st class.

1941 Jul: Laid down as *Mishima Maru* for the Kobe-Seattle service. Later intended as the *Aki Maru* for Australian service with accommodation for 90 1st class passengers and 206 3rd class passengers.
1942 May 15: Launched.
Oct 15: Delivered.
Entered service as a transport.
1944 Jul 26: The *Aki Maru* was torpedoed by the US submarine *Crevalle* west of Luzon and sank in position 18° 28′N-117° 59′E. 41 dead.

Motorship *Awa Maru*
Nippon Yusen KK, Tokyo

Builders: Mitsubishi, Nagasaki
Yard no: 770
11,249 GRT; 163.0 × 20.2 m /
535 × 66.3 ft; diesels, Mitsubishi;
Twin screw; 14,000 BHP; 20 kn;
Passengers: 137 1st class.

1942 Aug 24: Launched.
1943 Mar 5: Intended like her sister ship for the Japan-Australia service, the *Awa Maru* was fitted out as a transport by the Japanese government because of the war.
1944 Aug 19: Badly damaged by a torpedo from the US submarine *Rasher* near Luzon.
1945 Feb 1: The USA accepted Japan's application for diplomatic status for the *Awa Maru,* which was subsequently disarmed, painted green and marked with white crosses on the side.
Feb 27: Start of the voyage Moji-Kaohsiung-Hong Kong-Saigon-Singapore-Djakarta.

On board were 24,295 parcels for prisoners-of-war. However, most of the cargo consisted of war material. The Japanese had deliberately registered this large ship under the safe flag of the International Red Cross, in order to reach strongholds which were difficult to supply at that time and then to bring back valuable cargoes from those places.
Mar 28: On the return voyage the *Awa Maru* left Singapore for Tsuruga. As the ship, with its diplomatic status, was considered safe, passengers had streamed aboard until there was literally no space left. Over 2,000 people, including 17 women and children, wanted to make use of this last apparently safe opportunity of returning home. Another child was born aboard while the ship was at sea.
Apr 1: The US submarine *Queenfish* sighted the *Awa Maru,* and in the overcast weather took

her to be a warship. The submarine fired a quadruple torpedo salvo. Three minutes later, after the four detonations, the liner had sunk. Only one survivor was rescued by the *Queenfish*.
The position of the sinking is given by the US Navy as 25° 26′N-120° 08′E. Various Japanese attempts to locate the wreck failed, but serve as an indication of the inestimable value of the cargo. The Japanese government has, in any case, emphatically reserved for itself ownership of the wreck.

4/5 In December 1937 four more ships were ordered: the Miike Maru *(4) and* Mishima Maru *for the Kobe-Seattle service and the* Aki Maru *and* Awa Maru *(5) for the Kobe-Australia service. After war broke out between the USA and Japan the* Mishima Maru *was redesignated for the Australia service and renamed* Aki Maru*. A* Mishima Maru *was then to have been built as a fourth ship, but the order was cancelled because of a shortage of materials. It was for this reason that the* Aki Maru *and* Awa Maru *each had one superstructure deck less than planned.*
6 The Kashiwara Maru *and* Izumo Maru *were to have become the largest Japanese passenger ships ever built. However, both were taken over before completion by the Japanese Navy and subsequently lost during the war while serving as aircraft carriers. (Drawing by K.-H. Schwadtke.)*

Turbine steamer *Kashiwara Maru*
Nippon Yusen KK, Tokyo

1941 *Junyo*

Builders: Mitsubishi, Nagasaki
Yard no: 900
27,700 GRT; 220.0 × 26.7 m / 722 × 87.6 ft; Geared turbines, Mitsubishi; Twin screw; 56,250 SHP; 24, max 25.5 kn; Passengers: 220 1st class, 120 2nd class, 550 3rd class.

1939 Mar 20: Laid down as the largest and fastest passenger ship for the Yokohama-San Francisco route.
1940 Aug: The Japanese Navy took over the building contract and had the ship completed as an aircraft carrier under yard number 901.
1941 Jun 26: Launched as the *Junyo*.
1942 May 5: Delivered. Commissioned by the Japanese Navy.
1944 Dec 9: The *Junyo* was torpedoed by the US submarines *Redfish* and *Seadevil* east of Nagasaki. She was so badly damaged that she took no further part in the war.
1947 Broken up at Sasebo.

Turbine steamer *Izumo Maru*
Nippon Yusen KK, Tokyo

1941 *Hiyo*

Builders: Kawasaki, Kobe
27,500 GRT; 220.0 × 26.7 m / 722 × 87.6 ft; Geared turbines; twin screw; 56,250 SHP; 24, max 25.5 kn; Passengers: 220 1st class, 120 2nd class, 550 3rd class.

1939 Nov: Laid down. The ship was intended for the trans-Pacific Yokohama-San Francisco service like her sister ship *Kashiwara Maru*.
1940 Aug: The building contract was taken over by the Japanese Navy. The ship was to be completed as an aircraft carrier.
1941 Jun 24: Launched as the *Hiyo*.
1942 Jul 31: Commissioned by the Japanese Navy.
1943 Jun 10: Badly damaged by a torpedo from the US submarine *Trigger*.
1944 Jun 20: The *Hiyo* was attacked by aircraft from the US aircraft carrier *Belleau Wood* 450 nautical miles northwest of Yap and sank in position 15° 30′N-133° 50′E.

6

The America

Turbine steamer *America*
United States Lines, New York

1942 *West Point*
1946 *America*
1964 *Australis*

Builders: Newport News SB & DD Co
Yard no: 369
26,454 GRT; 220.4 × 28.4 m / 723 × 93.2 ft; Parsons geared turbines from builders; Twin screw; 37,400 SHP; 22, max over 24 kn; passengers: 543 cabin class, 418 tourist class, 241 3rd class; Crew: 643.

1939 Aug 31: Launched.
1940 Jul 2: Delivered. The ship had been intended for the North Atlantic service, but because of the war in Europe was used for cruising in American waters.

Aug 10: First cruise New York-West Indies.
1941 Taken over by the US Navy and fitted out as a troop transport.
1942 Renamed *Westpoint*.
1946 Jul 22: Discharged from transport service. Renamed *America*. Overhauled by builders. 26,314 GRT. Passengers: 516 1st class, 371 cabin class, 159 tourist class.
1946 Nov 14: First voyage in Transatlantic service New York-Le Havre.
1951 Oct 25: Service extended to Bremerhaven.
1960 Measurement 33,961 GRT. Passengers: 516 1st class, 530 tourist class.
1964 Nov: Sold to D & A Chandris Piraeus. Renamed *Australis*. Registered for Okeania SA,

Piraeus. Refitted at Piraeus as a one-class ship for 2,300 passengers. 26,485 GRT.
1965 Aug 20: First voyage Piraeus-Sydney.
Oct 16: First voyage in round-the-world service Southampton-Mediterranean-Australia-New Zealand-Southampton.
1968 26,315 GRT.

1/2 Completed in 1940 as the flagship of the United States Lines, the America *(1) was taken over by the US Navy after a few cruises and commissioned as the troop transport* West Point *(2).*
3 In 1964 the ship was sold to Chandris to become the Australis.

Turbo-electric vessel *Vaterland*
Hamburg-America Line,
Hamburg

Builders: Blohm & Voss,
Hamburg
Yard no: 523
41,000 GRT; 251.2 × 30.0 m /
824 × 98.4 ft; Turbo-electric
engines, SSW-B & V; Twin screw;
62,000 SHP; 23.5, max 25.5 kn;
Passengers: 354 1st class, 435
tourist class, 533 3rd class.

1940 Aug 24: Launched. The ship
was intended for the Hamburg-
America Line's North Atlantic
service and for cruising during the
winter. Laid up incomplete
because of the war at the builders'
yard in the Kuhwerder harbour.
1943 Jul 25: During the heavy air
raids on Hamburg, the *Vaterland*
was hit by several bombs and
completely burnt out.

1948 The wreck was broken up at
Hamburg.

*1/2 The launching of no 523 by Blohm
& Voss.*
*3 This was to have been the appearance
of the* Vaterland *after completion.*

In 1941 the British Ministry of War Transport decided to fit out some fast cargo liners with simple passenger accommodation, temporary for the duration of the war. This was in order to maintain a minimum number of berths in the face of the shortage caused by the diversion of passenger ships to other duties. The first ship was the *Beaverhill,* which in 1941 was fitted with cabins for 138 passengers followed by the newly-built *Empire Grace* in 1942. After this there were no more ships fitted out by the MoWT, but after the war the idea was taken up by British shipowners trying to ease the bottleneck in passenger berths. Three new ships were completed in this way; by 1950 the accommodation had been removed.

Turbine steamer *Beaverhill*
Canadian Pacific, London

Builders: Barclay, Curle & Co, Glasgow
Yard no: 618
10,041 GRT; 159.3 × 18.8 m / 523 × 61.7 ft; Geared turbines, Parsons; Single screw; 8,000 SHP; 14 kn; Passengers: 138 in one class.

1927 Nov 8: Launched.
1928 Feb: Completed as a cargo vessel without passenger accommodation.
Feb 18: Maiden voyage Glasgow-Canada.
1940 The *Beaverhill* remained on her old route during the war, but under the management of the Ministry of War Transport.
1941 Oct: The ship was given accommodation for 138

passengers.
1944 Nov 24: The *Beaverhill* stranded on Hillyards Reef off St John. Attempts to refloat her failed, and she had to be abandoned.
1946 Dec 11: The stern section was successfully salvaged, but sank again in the harbour of St John. When it had been refloated, it was towed out to sea and sunk off the Grand Manan Island.

1 *The Canadian Pacific cargo liner* Beaverhill *was given passenger accommodation in 1941.*

1

Motorship *Empire Grace*
Shaw, Savill & Albion,
Southampton

1946 *Wairangi*

Builders: Harland & Wolff,
Belfast
Yard no: 1051
13,478 GRT; 164.6 × 21.4 m /
540 × 70.2 ft; H & W diesels;
Twin screw; 16,000 BHP; 17 kn;
Passengers: 112 tourist class.

1942 Apr: Completed for the
MoWT; Shaw, Savill & Albion
Line took over the management.
Entered Great Britain-New
Zealand-Australia service.
1946 Sold to Shaw, Savill &
Albion. Renamed *Wairangi*.
1951 Passenger accommodation
removed except for 12 berths.
12,804 GRT.
1963 Aug 14: Stranded 25
nautical miles off Stockholm.
Aug 26: Refloated.
To Faslane to be broken up.

Motorship *Port Hobart*
Port Line, London

Launched as *Empire Wessex*

Builders: Harland & Wolff,
Belfast
Yard no: 1188
11,877 GRT; 164.6 × 21.4 m /
540 × 70.2 ft; H & W diesels;
Twin screw; 16,000 BHP; 17 kn;
Passengers: 36 1st class, 92 tourist
class.

1946 Launched as the *Empire
Wessex* for the MoWT.
Aug: Completed as *Port Hobart*.
London-Australia-New Zealand
service.
Passenger accommodation
removed in 1950 except for 12 1st
class berths.
1970 Arrived at Shanghai; broken
up there.

Motorship *Empire Star*
Blue Star Line, London

Launched as *Empire Mercia*
Builders: Harland & Wolff,
Belfast
Yard no: 1303
11,861 GRT; 164.6 × 21.4 m /
540 × 70.2 ft: H & W diesels;

Twin screw; 16,000 BHP; 17 kn;
Passengers: 36 1st class, 92 tourist
class.

1946 Launched as *Empire Mercia*
for the MoWT.
Dec: Completed as *Empire Star*.
1947 Jan: Maiden voyage
Glasgow-South Africa-Australia.
1950 Accommodation for only 12
1st class passengers.
1971 Oct 16: Arrived at
Kaohsiung to be broken up.

Motorship *Port Pirie*
Port Line, London

Builders: Swan, Hunter &
Wigham Richardson, Newcastle
Yard no: 1741
10,561 GRT; 161.2 × 20.8 m /
529 × 68.2 ft; Doxford diesels
from builders; Twin screw; 10,700
BHP; 16 kn; Passengers: 48 in one
class.

1947 Completed; entered London-
Australia-New Zealand service.
1950/1951 Passenger
accommodation reduced to 12 1st
class.
1972 Jul 2: Arrived at Castellon to
be broken up by V. Davalillo.

2

2 *The* Empire Grace *undergoing trials (1942) in wartime grey.*
3 *The* Port Hobart *on the Elbe in 1969.*
4 *The launching of the* Empire Mercia *at the Harland & Wolff yard.*
5 *The* Port Pirie.

3

4

American Troop Transports

This section deals with the six classes of US standard ships which measured more than 10,000 GRT, and which were built as troop transports during the Second World War. Although very few of these ships were ever used in civilian passenger service, they share similar characteristics with passenger vessels, for which reason they have been included without exception in this work. Due to the sometimes very large number of ships in any one class, the technical details have been placed together under each class heading.

Class C3-IN-P&C (4 Ships)

149.0 × 21.1 m / 489 × 69.2 ft; Geared turbines; Single screw; 8,750 SHP; 16.5 kn; Accommodation for 2,000 troops. Builders: Ingalls, Pascagoula

Turbine steamer *Pascagoula*
US Government

1942 *George W. Goethals*

12,093 GRT; Yard no: 268

1941 Jan 7: Laid down as *American Merchant* for United States Lines, New York. Intended for the New York-London service with accommodation for 165 passengers. Taken over by the US Government before launching.
1942 Jan 23: Launched as *Pascagoula*.
Sep 18: Delivered. Renamed *George W. Goethals* on the same day and commissioned by the US Army.
1946 Refitted as a troop transport to peacetime standards by Todd Shipy Corp. Accommodation for 273 adults and 179 children.
1948 Again refitted by Atlantic Basin Iron Works at Brooklyn to improve fire safety. Now 360 passengers.

1950 Mar 1: Handed over to the US Navy. Entered the Military Sea Transportation service. Type Designation number: T-AP 182.
1960 Nov 20: Handed over to the Maritime Administration. Allotted to the reserve fleet and laid up near Jones Point in the Hudson.
1970 Dec 31: Arrived in tow at Castellon. Broken up there by I. Varela.

Turbine steamer *Biloxi*
US Government

1943 *Henry Gibbins*
1960 *Empire State IV*

12,090 GRT; Yard no: 297

1941 Laid down as *American Banker* for United States Lines. Intended for the London-New York service. 165 passengers.
1942 Nov 11: Launched as *Biloxi* for the US Government.
Feb 27: Completed. Renamed *Henry Gibbins* on the same day and commissioned by the US Army as a troop transport.
1946 Refitted as a troop transport to peacetime standards by Gibbins Engine & Machine Co, Boston. 275 adults, 180 children.
1949 Fire safety improved during refit at Atl Basin Iron Works, Brooklyn. 360 passengers.
1950 Mar 1: To US Navy. Entered the MSTS. Type Designation number T-AP 183.
1959 Dec 2: Handed over to the Maritime Administration.
1960 Made available to the New York State Maritime College at Fort Schuyler as a training ship. Renamed *Empire State IV*.

1

2

1 *The* George W. Goethals *ex*
Pascagoula *as an MSTS transport.*
2 *The* Biloxi *has been serving since
1960 as the training ship* Empire State
IV.

Turbine steamer *Gulfport*
US Government

1943 *David C. Shanks*

12,097 GRT; Yard no: 298

1942 Laid down as *American Farmer* for United States Lines. Intended for New York-London service, 165 passengers.
1942 Aug 22: Launched as *Gulfport* for the US Government.
1943 Apr 24: Delivered. Renamed *David C. Shanks* on the same day and commissioned as troop transport by the US army.
1946 Refitted as peacetime troop transport at San Francisco. Passengers: 275 adults, 180 children, 678 soldiers.
1947 Refitted by Bethlehem at San Francisco to improve fire safety.
1950 Placed in the MSTS by the US Navy. Type Designation number: T-AP 180.
1960 Handed over to the Maritime Administration. Allotted to the reserve fleet and laid up in Suisun bay at San Francisco.
1973 Mar 1: Sold to D.L. Hewitt at Los Angeles to be broken up. The sale fell through due to breach of contract on the part of the buyer.
Jun 26: Sold to the Inter Ocean Grain Storage Co, Washington.
Nov: Arrived at Kaohsiung to be broken up.

Turbine steamer *Pass Christian*
US Government

1943 *Fred C. Ainsworth*

12,093 GRT; Yard no: 299

1942 Laid down as *American Shipper* for United States Lines. Intended for New York-London service with accommodation for 165 passengers.
Sep 12: Launched as *Pass Christian* for the US Government.
1943 Jun 4: Delivered. Renamed *Fred C. Ainsworth* on the same day and commissioned by the US Army as a troop transport.
1946 Refitted as a troop transport at San Francisco to peacetime standards. Accommodation for 426 passengers and 687 troops.
1950 Mar 1: Placed in the MSTS by the US Navy. Type Designation number T-AP 181.
1959 Nov 2: Handed over to the Maritime Administration. Allotted to the reserve fleet and laid up in Suisun Bay, San Francisco.
1973 Mar 1: Sold to D.L. Hewitt, Los Angeles, to be broken up. The sale fell through due to a breach of contract on the part of the buyer.
Jun 26: Sold to the Inter Ocean Grain Storage Co, Washington.
Nov 4: Arrived at Kaohsiung to be broken up.

3 *The* David C. Shanks *ex* Gulfport.

3

150.0 × 21.1 m / 492 × 69.2 ft; Geared turbines; Single screw; 9,350 SHP; 17 kn.

Builders: Seattle-Tacoma SB Co, Tacoma

Turbine steamer *Frederick Funston*
US Army

11,971 GRT; Yard no: 6

1941 Sep 27: Launched.

1942 Oct 28: Delivered.
1943 Apr 8: Handed over to the US Navy. Type Designation number AP 48, later APA 89.
1946 Apr: Returned to the US Army. Refitted as troop transport to peacetime standards.
1950 Apr 28: Placed in MSTS by the US Navy. Number: T-AP 178.
1960 To the Maritime Administration. Consigned to the reserve fleet and laid up.

Turbine steamer *James O'Hara*
US Army

11,971 GRT; Yard no: 7

1941 Dec 30: Launched.
Nov 30: Delivered.
1943 Apr 15: Handed over to the US Navy. Number: AP 49, later APA 90.
1946 Apr 5: Returned to the US Army. Refitted as troop transport to peacetime standards.
1950 Placed in the MSTS by the US Navy. Number: T-AP 179.
1960 Jan 14: Laid up by the Maritime Administration.

1/2 *The* Frederick Funston *at the builders' yard shortly before delivery in April 1943 (1) and the* James O'Hara *as a US Army transport in the '50s (2).*

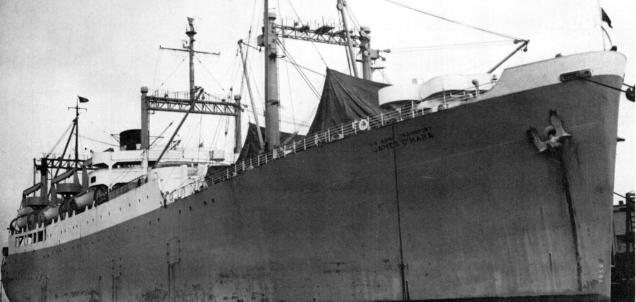

1

2

94 Class C4-S-A1 (30 Ships)

10,654 GRT.
159.3 × 21.7 m / 523 × 71.2 ft;
Geared turbines, Westinghouse;
Single screw; 9,900 SHP; 17 kn;
Accommodation for up to 3,000
troops; Crew: 256.
Builders: Kaiser, Richmond/Cal.

Turbine steamer *General G.O.
Squier*
US Navy

1964 *Pennmar*

Yard no: 1

1942 Nov 11: Launched.
1943 Oct 2: Commissioned.
Number AP 130.
Oct 29: Maiden voyage.
1946 Jul 18: Laid up in the reserve
fleet on the James River.
1964 Apr 7: Sold to the Bethlehem
Steel Corp. Rebuilt at Baltimore as
a cargo vessel. Renamed *Pennmar*.
11,538 GRT.
1965 Jan: Entered service as a
cargo vessel. Managed by Calmar
SS Co, Wilmington/Del.
1974 Sold to Calmar.
1975 Feb 22: Laid up in
Baltimore.

1976 Aug: Sold to an American
corporation.

Turbine steamer *General T.H.
Bliss*
US Navy

1964 *Seamar*
1975 *Caroni*

Yard no: 2

1942 Dec 19: Launched.
1944 Feb 24: Commissioned.
Number AP 131.
Mar 27: Maiden voyage San
Francisco-New Caledonia.
1946 Jul 2: Laid up at Olympia/
Wash. Reserve fleet.
1964 Apr: Sold to the Bethlehem
Steel Corp. Rebuilt at Sparrows
Point as a cargo vessel. Renamed
Seamar. 11,538 GRT.
Managed by Calmar SS Co,
Wilmington/Del.
1974 Sold to Calmar.
1975 Sold to Cia An Venezolana
de Nav, Caracas. Renamed
Caroni.

Turbine steamer *General J.R.
Brooke*
US Navy

1964 *Marymar*

Yard no: 3

1943 Feb 21: Launched.
1944 Jan 20: Commissioned.
Number AP 132.
Feb 24: Maiden voyage Port
Hueneme-Pearl Harbour.
1946 Jul 18: Laid up on James
River. Reserve fleet.
1964 Apr: Sold to the Bethlehem
Steel Corp. Rebuilt at Baltimore as
a cargo vessel. Renamed
Marymar. 11,513 GRT.
1965 In service. Managed by
Calmar SS Co, Wilmington/Del.
1974 Sold to Calmar.
1975 Nov 25: Laid up in
Baltimore.
1976 Aug: Sold to an American
corporation.

1 General G.O. Squier, *photograph
1943*.
2 General T.H. Bliss, *photograph
March 1944*.
3 *USNT* General J.R. Brooke.

1

2

3

Turbine steamer *General O.H. Ernst*
US Navy

1964 *Calmar*
1975 *Orinoco*

Yard no: 4

1943 Apr 14: Launched.
1944 Apr 22: Commissioned. Number AP 133.
Aug 27: Maiden voyage Seattle-Honolulu.
1946 Aug 15: Laid up in Suisun Bay. Reserve fleet.
1964 Apr: Sold to the Bethlehem Steel Corp. Rebuilt at San Francisco as a cargo vessel. Renamed *Calmar*. 11,424 GRT. Managed by Calmar SS Co, Wilmington/Del.
1974 Sold to Calmar.
1975 Sold to Cia An. Venezolana de Nav, Caracas. Renamed *Orinoco*.

Turbine steamer *General R.L. Howze*
US Navy

1969 *Guam Bear*
1975 *New Zealand Bear*
1976 *Austral Glen*

Yard no: 5

1943 May 23: Launched.
1944 Feb 7: Commissioned. Number AP 134.
Mar 20: Maiden voyage San Francisco-New Guinea.
1946 To the US Army. Laid up until 1948. 12,544 GRT.
1950 Mar 1: To the US Navy for MSTS. Number: T-AP 134.
1958 Jul 17: Laid up at Astoria, Oregon, by the Maritime Administration.
1968 Sold to the Pacific Far East Line Inc, San Francisco.
Apr 19: Rebuilding as container ship commenced by Todd Shipyard, Alameda.
1969 May: In service as *Guam Bear*. 11,444 GRT.
1975 Renamed *New Zealand Bear*.
1976 To Farrel Lines Inc, New York. Renamed *Austral Glen*.

Turbine steamer *General W.M. Black*
US Navy

1967 *Green Forest*

Yard no: 6

1943 Jul 23: Launched.
1944 Feb 24: Commissioned. Number AP 135.
Mar 26: Maiden voyage San Francisco-Pearl Habour.
1946 Feb 28: Handed over to US Army. 12,551 GRT.
1950 Mar 1: Returned to US Navy. Entered MSTS. Number: T-AP 135.
1955 To Maritime Administration. Laid up in Suisun Bay.
1967 Sold to Central Gulf SS Corp, New Orleans.
May: Rebuilding as cargo vessel commenced by Tampa Ship Repair & DD Co.
Renamed *Green Forest*.
1968 Jun: In service. 10,577 GRT.

4 *USNT* General O.H. Ernst.
5 *USAT* General R.L. Howze.
6 *USNT* General W.M. Black.

4

U. S. N. S.
GENERAL W. M. BLACK

Turbine steamer *General H.L. Scott*
US Navy

1964 *Yorkmar*
1974 *Yorkmaru*

Yard no: 7

1943 Sep 19: Launched.
1944 Apr 3: Commissioned.
Number AP 136.
May 5: Maiden voyage San Francisco-Pacific.
1946 Jun: Laid up in the reserve fleet in Puget Sound.
1964 Sold to Bethlehem Steel Corp.
Mar: Rebuilding as cargo vessel commenced at Baltimore.
Renamed *Yorkmar*.
1965 In service. Managed by Calmar SS Co, Wilmington/Del.
11,421 GRT.
1974 Sold to Calmar. Sold again to Hou Yung SS Co which renamed her *Yorkmaru,* and sold her to Spanish shipbreakers.

Turbine steamer *General Harry Taylor*
US Navy

1963 *General Hoyt S. Vandenberg*

Yard no: 8

1943 Oct 10: Launched.
1944 May 8: Commissioned.
Number AP 145.
Jun 23: Maiden voyage San Francisco-Milne Bay.
1946 Handed over to US Army.
12,544 GRT.
1950 Mar 1: Returned to Navy.
Entered MSTS. Number: T-AP 145.
1958 Jul 10: To the Maritime Administration. Laid up in the reserve fleet at Beaumont, Texas.
1962/63 Rebuilt as satellite tracking ship by Bethlehem Steel Corp.
1963 Jul 18: Commissioned by US Air Force at Baltimore as *General Hoyt S. Vandenberg.*
1964 Jul: Handed over to US Navy. Number: T-AGM 10.

Turbine steamer *General S.D. Sturgis*
US Navy

1967 *Green Port*

Yard no: 9

1943 Nov 12: Launched.
1944 Jul 10: Commissioned.
Number: AP 137.
Aug 18: Maiden voyage Seattle-Honolulu.
1946 Jun 24: Handed over to US Army. 12,349 GRT.
1950 Returned to US Navy.
Entered MSTS. Number: T-AP 137.
1958 Aug 22: To the Maritime Administration. Laid up in the reserve fleet at Beaumont, Texas.
1967 Sold to Central Gulf SS Corp, New Orleans. Renamed *Green Port.*
Dec: Rebuilding as cargo vessel commenced by Tampa Ship Repair & DD Co.
1968 Jun: In service. 10,573 GRT.

7 General H.L. Scott, *1944 photograph.*

8 *USAT* General Harry Taylor.
9 General S.D. Sturgis, *May 1944 photograph.*

7

Turbine steamer *General W.F. Hase*
US Navy

1969 *Transidaho*
1975 *Carolina*

Yard no: 10

1943 Dec 15: Launched.
1944 Jun 6: Commissioned. Number AP 146.
Jul 15: Maiden voyage San Francisco-Pearl Harbour.
1946 Jun: Handed over to US Army. 12,551 GRT.
1950 Returned to US Navy. Entered MSTS. Number: T-AP 146.
1960 Jan 8: Laid up by the Maritime Administration in the reserve fleet in Suisun Bay.
1968 Sold to Hudson Waterways Corp, New York.
Aug 31: Rebuilding as container ship commenced by Maryland SB & DD Co, Baltimore.
1969 Renamed *Transidaho*.
1970 In service. 13,489 GRT. Length overall 192.9 m / 633 ft.
1975 To the Puerto Rico Marit Shipping Authority, San Juan, as the *Carolina*.

Turbine steamer *General E.T. Collins*
US Navy

1969 *New Orleans*
1975 *Guayama*

Yard no: 11

1944 Jan 22: Launched.
Jul 20: Commissioned. Number AP 147.
Aug 14: Maiden voyage San Diego-Pacific.
1946 Jun: Handed over to the Army. 13,000 GRT.
1950 Placed in MSTS by US Navy. Number: T-AP 147.
1960 Jun 30: To the Maritime Administration. Laid up in the reserve fleet in Suisun Bay.
1968 Sold to Containership Chartering Service, Wilmington/Del. Rebuilt as container ship by Willamette Iron & Steel Co, Portland/Or.
1969 Mar: Entered service as *New Orleans*. 11,400 GRT.
1975 Sold as the *Guayama* to the Puerto Rico Marit Shipping Authority, San Juan.

Turbine steamer *General M.L. Hersey*
US Navy

1968 *St. Louis*

Yard no: 12

1944 Apr 1: Launched.
Jul 29: Commissioned. Number AP 148.
Sep 5: Maiden voyage San Francisco-New Guinea.
1946 Jun: Handed over to the Army. 12,326 GRT.
1950 Place in MSTS by the Navy. Number: T-AP 148.
1951 Nov 4: The *General M.L. Hersey* collided in the mouth of the Elbe with the Argentinian passenger ship *Maipu,* which was badly damaged and sank.
1959 Sep 3: To the Maritime Administration. Laid up in the reserve fleet in Suisun Bay.
1968 Sold to Sea Land Service Inc, Wilmington/Del: Renamed *St. Louis*.
Sep 16: Rebuilding as container vessel commenced at Galveston.
1969 Dec: In service. 11,522 GRT.
1970 New, longer forepart fitted. 18,362 GRT. Length overall 211.8 m / 695 ft. Breadth: 23.8 m / 78.1 ft.

10 General E.T. Collins, *photograph June 1947.*
11 *USAT* General M.L. Hersey.

Turbine steamer *General J.H. McRae*
US Navy

1969 *Transhawaii*
1975 *Aguadilla*

Yard no: 14

1944 Apr 26: Launched.
Aug 8: Commissioned. Number AP 149.
Sep 20: Maiden voyage San Francisco-Honolulu.
1946 Feb 27: Handed over to US Army. 12,496 GRT.
1950 Placed in MSTS by US Navy. Number: T-AP 149.
1960 Jun 30: Laid up by Maritime Administration in reserve fleet in Suisun Bay.
1968 Sold to Hudson Waterways Corp, New York.
Aug 29: Rebuilding as container vessel commenced at Baltimore by Maryland SB & DD Co.
1969 Renamed *Transhawaii*
1970 In service. 13,489 GRT.
192.9 m / 633 ft length overall.
1975 To the Puerto Rico Maritime Shipping Authority as *Aguadilla*.

Turbine steamer *General C.G. Morton*
US Navy

1967 *Green Wave*

Yard no: 12

1944 May: Launched.
Jul 7: Commissioned. Number: AP 138.
Aug: Maiden voyage San Pedro-Guadalcanal.
1946 May: Handed over to US Army. 12,444 GRT.
1950 Returned to US Navy for MSTS service.
1958 May 29: Laid up in reserve fleet by Maritime Administration.
1967 Sold to Central Gulf SS Corp, New Orleans.
May: Rebuilding as cargo vessel commenced by Tampa Ship Repair & DD Co. Renamed *Green Wave*.
1968 Jun: In service. 10,562 GRT.

Turbine steamer *General R.E. Callan*
US Navy

1963 *General H.H. Arnold*

Yard no: 15

1944 Apr 27: Launched.
Aug 17: Commissioned. Number: AP 139.
Sep 25: Maiden voyage San Francisco-New Guinea.
1946 May 24: Handed over to US Army. 12,351 GRT.
1950 Returned to US Navy for MSTS service. Number: T-AP 139.
1958 Jul 17: Laid up in reserve fleet by Maritime Administration.
1962/63 Rebuilt as satellite tracking ship by Bethlehem Steel Corp.
1963 Renamed *General H.H. Arnold* and commissioned by US Air Force.
1964 Handed over to US Navy. Number: T-AGM 9.

12 *USNT* General J.H. McRae.

12

13 General C.G. Morton, *photograph December 1947*.
14 *USNT* General R.E. Callan.

Turbine steamer *General M.M. Patrick*
US Navy

1968 *Boston*

Yard no: 16

1944 Jun 21: Launched.
Sep 4: Commissioned. Number: AP 150.
Oct 14: Maiden voyage San Francisco-Pearl Harbour.
1946 Mar 11: Handed over to US Army. 12,544 GRT.
1950 Commissioned by US Navy for MSTS. Number: T-AP 150.
1958 Oct 17: To the Maritime Administration. Laid up in the reserve fleet at Olympia.
1967 Sold to Litton Industries Leasing Corp, Wilmington/Del.
Sep: Rebuilding as container vessel commenced by Todd Shipyard at Galveston.
1968 Jul: Entered service in Sea Land Services as the *Boston*.
1975 Sold to be broken up in the USA.

Turbine steamer *General W.C. Langfitt*
US Navy

1969 *Transindiana*

Yard no: 17

1944 Jul 17: Launched.
Sep 30: Commissioned. Number: AP 151.
Nov 10: Maiden voyage San Diego-Eniwetok.
1946 Jun: Handed over to US Army. 12,544 GRT.
1950 Returned to US Navy and MSTS service. Number: T-AP 151.
1958 May 13: Laid up by Maritime Administration in reserve fleet in James River.
1968 Sold to Hudson Waterways Corp, New York. Rebuilt as container vessel by Maryland SB & DD Co at Baltimore.
1969 Dec: Entered service as *Transindiana*. 13,489 GRT.
Length overall 192.9 m / 633 ft.

Turbine steamer *General Omar Bundy*
US Navy

1964 *Portmar*

Yard no: 18

1944 Aug 5: Launched.
1945 Jan 6: Commissioned. Number: AP 152.
Mar 10: Maiden voyage San Francisco-Pacific.
1946 Aug 30: US Army.
1949 Dec 12: US Dept of Commerce. Laid up in reserve fleet in James River.
1964 Apr 10: Sold to Bethlehem Steel Corp. Renamed *Portmar*.
Aug: Rebuilding as cargo vessel commenced at Baltimore.
1965 In service. Managed by Calmar SS Co, Wilmington/Del. 11,421 GRT.
1974 Sold to Calmar.
1976 Aug: Sold to an American corporation.

15 General M.M. Patrick, *photograph February 1948.*

15

16 *USNT* General W.C. Langfitt.
17 *USAT* General Omar Bundy.

Turbine steamer *General R.M. Blatchford*
US Navy

1970 *Stonewall Jackson*
1973 *Alex Stephens*

Yard no: 19

1944 Aug 27: Launched.
1945 Jan 26: Commissioned.
Number: AP 153.
Mar 12: Maiden voyage San Francisco-Manila.
1946 Jun: Handed over to US Army. 13,100 GRT.
1950 Returned to US Navy. Entered MSTS. Number: T-AP 153.
1968 Sep 17: Handed over to Maritime Administration. Laid up.
1969 Jan: Sold to Waterman Carriers Inc, New York. Rebuilding as container ship commenced by Albina E & M Work at Portland.
1970 Renamed *Stonewall Jackson* and entered service. 10,562 GRT.
1973 Renamed *Alex Stephens*.

Turbine steamer *General Le Roy Eltinge*
US Navy

1969 *Robert E. Lee*
1973 *Robert Toombs*

Yard no: 20

1944 Sep 20: Launched.
1945 Feb 21: Commissioned.
Number: AP 154.
Mar 23: Maiden voyage San Diego-Calcutta.
1946 Jun: Handed over to the US Army. 13,100 GRT.
1950 Taken over by the US Navy again for MSTS service. Number: T-AP 154.
1968 Sep 17: Handed over to the Maritime Administration. Laid up.
1969 Jan: Sold to Waterman Carriers Inc, New York. Rebuilding as container vessel commenced by Albina E & M Work, Portland.
Dec: Renamed *Robert E. Lee* and entered service. 10,562 GRT.
1973 Sep: Renamed *Robert Toombs*.

Turbine steamer *General M.B. Stewart*
US Navy

1967 *Albany*
1974 *Mission Viking*

Yard no: 21

1944 Oct 15: Launched.
1945 Mar 3: Commissioned.
Number: AP 140.
Apr 2: Maiden voyage San Francisco-Pearl Harbour.
1946 May: Handed over to the US Army. 12,521 GRT.
1950 Taken over by the US Navy again for MSTS service. Number: T-AP 140.
1958 May 21: Handed over to the Maritime Administration and laid up in reserve fleet in the Hudson.
1967 Sold to Albany River Transport Inc, New York.
Jun: Rebuilding as cargo vessel commenced by Todd Shipyard, Brooklyn. Renamed *Albany*.
1968 Dec: In service after rebuilding work. 10,530 GRT.
1974 Sold to Avondale Shipyards Inc as *Mission Viking*.

18

18 *USAT* General R.M. Blatchford.
19 *USNT* General Le Roy Eltinge.
20 *USNT* General M.B. Stewart.

Turbine steamer *General A. W. Greely*
US Navy

1969 *Hawaii Bear*
1976 *Austral Glade*

Yard no: 22

1944 Nov 5: Launched.
1945 Mar 22: Commissioned.
Number AP 141.
Apr 16: Maiden voyage San Pedro-Australia.
1946 Mar 20: Handed over to the US Army. 12,665 GRT.
1950 Returned to the US Navy for MSTS service. Number: T-AP 141.
1959 Aug 29: Handed over to the Maritime Administration and laid up in the reserve fleet at Olympia/Wash.
1968 Sold to Pacific Far East Line Inc, San Francisco.
Apr 19: Rebuilding as container vessel commenced by Todd Shipyard, Alameda.
1969 May: Entered service as *Hawaii Bear*. 11,447 GRT.
1975 Sold to Farrell Lines Inc, New York.
1976 Renamed *Austral Glade*.

Turbine steamer *General C.H. Muir*
US Navy

1969 *Chicago*
1975 *San Juan*

Yard no: 23

1944 Nov 24: Launched.
1945 Apr 12: Commissioned.
Number: AP 142.
May 13: Maiden voyage San Francisco-Pearl Harbour.
1946 Jun 18: Handed over to the US Army. 13,000 GRT.
1950 Taken over by the US Navy again for MSTS. Number: T-AP 142.
1960 Jun 30: Laid up by Maritime Administration in the reserve fleet in Suisun Bay.
1968 Sold to Sea Land Services Inc, Wilmington/Del. Rebuilt as container vessel by Todd Shipyard, Galveston.
1969 Entered service as *Chicago*. 18,455 GRT. Length overall 211.8 m / 695 ft, breadth 23.8 m / 78.1 ft.
1975 To Puerto Rico Maritime Shipping Authority, San Juan. Renamed *San Juan*.

Turbine steamer *General H.B. Freeman*
US Navy

1968 *Newark*

Yard no: 24

1944 Dec 11: Launched.
1945 Apr 26: Commissioned.
Number: AP 143.
Jun 1: Maiden voyage San Diego-Calcutta.
1946 Mar: Handed over to the US Army. 12,544 GRT.
1950 Taken over by the US Navy again for MSTS service. Number: T-AP 143.
1958 Laid up by the Maritime Administration in reserve fleet at Olympia.
1967 Sold to Madison Transportation Co Inc, Wilmington/Del.
Sep: Rebuilding as container vessel commenced by Todd Shipyard, Galveston.
1968 Jun: Entered Sea Land Services as *Newark*. 11,389 GRT.

21 *The* General A.W. Greely, *photograh January 1948.*
22 *USNT* General C.H. Muir.

Turbine steamer *General H.F. Hodges*
US Navy

1968 *James*

Yard no: 25

1945 Jan 3: Launched.
Apr 6: Commissioned. Number: AP 144.
May 10: Maiden voyage San Francisco-Far East.
1946 May: To the US Army. 12,521 GRT.
1950 Mar 1: Returned to the US Navy for MSTS service. Number: T-AP 144.
1958 Jun 16: Laid up by the Maritime Administration on the Hudson.
1967 Sold to James River Transport Inc, New York.
Jul: Rebuilding commenced by Todd Shipyard, Brooklyn.
1968 Feb: Entered service as *James*. 10,530 GRT.

Turbine steamer *General A. W. Brewster*
US Navy

1968 *Philadelphia*

Yard no: 26

1945 Jan 21: Launched.
Apr 23: Commissioned. Number: AP 155.
May 28: Maiden voyage San Pedro-Avonmouth.
1946 Apr: Handed over to the US Army. 13,000 GRT.
1950 Mar 1: Returned to the US Navy for MSTS service. Number: T-AP 155.
1955 Jul 26: Laid up by the Maritime Administration in Suisan Bay.
1968 Sold to Sea Land Service Inc, Wilmington/Del.
Oct 10: Rebuilding as container vessel commenced by Bethlehem Steel at Baltimore. Renamed *Philadelphia*. 10,979 GRT.

Turbine steamer *General D.E. Aultman*
US Navy

1968 *Portland*

Yard no: 27

1945 Feb 18: Launched.
May 20: Commissioned. Number: AP 156.
Jul 1: Maiden voyage San Diego-Marseille.
1946 Mar: Sold to the US Army. 12,551 GRT.
1950 Mar 1: Returned to the US Navy for MSTS service. Number: T-AP 156.
1958 Jun 4: Laid up by the Maritime Administration in Suisun Bay.
1967 Sold to Containership Chartering Service, Wilmington/Del.
Oct: Rebuilding commenced as container vessel by Willamette Iron & Steel Co.
1968 Entered service as *Portland*. 11,389 GRT.

23 *USNT* General H.F. Hodges.
24 *USAT* General A.W. Brewster.

U. S. Army Transport
GENERAL A. W. BREWSTER

Turbine steamer *General C.C. Ballou*

1968 *Brooklyn*
1975 *Humacao*

Yard no: 28

1945 Mar 7: Launched.
Jun 30: Commissioned. Number: AP 157.
Jul 29: Maiden voyage San Diego-Marseille.
1946 May: To the US Army. 12,666 GRT.
1950 Mar 1: Returned to the US Navy for MSTS service. Number: T-AP 157.
1960 Jun 1: Laid up by the Maritime Administration at Beaumont.
1968 Sold to Sea Land Service Inc, Wilmington/Del. Rebuilt as container vessel by Alabama SB & DD Co. Renamed *Brooklyn*. 11,369 GRT.
1975 To Puerto Rico Shipping Authority, San Juan, as *Humacao*.

Turbine stamer *General W.G. Haan*
US Navy

1969 *Transoregon*
1975 *Mayaguez*

Yard no: 29

1945 Mar 20: Launched.
Aug 2: Commissioned. Number: AP 158.
Sep 4: Maiden voyage San Diego-East Asia.
1946 Jun: US Army. 12,511 GRT.
1950 Mar 1: Returned to the US Navy for MSTS service. Number: T-AP 158.
1958 Oct 22: Laid up by Maritime Administration at Beaumont.
1968 Sold to Hudson Waterways Corp, New York. Rebuilt as container vessel by Maryland SB & DD Co, Baltimore.
1969 Dec: Entered service as *Transoregon*. 13,489 GRT. Length overall 192.9 m / 633 ft.
1975 To Puerto Rico Maritime Shipping Authority as *Mayaguez*.

Turbine steamer *General Stuart Heintzelmann*
US Navy

1968 *Mobile*

Yard no: 30

1945 Apr 21: Launched.
Sep 12: Commissioned. Number: AP 159.
Oct 9: Maiden voyage San Diego-Yokohama.
1946 Jun: US Army. 12,666 GRT.
1950 Returned to the US Navy for MSTS service. Number: T-AP 159.
1960 Jun: Laid up in reserve fleet by the Maritime Administration.
1968 Sold to Sea Land Services Inc, Wilmington/Del.
May 2: Rebuilding commenced as container vessel by Alabama SB & DD Co. Renamed *Mobile*.
1969 Jan: Entered service. 11,302 GRT.

25 *USAT* General C.C. Ballou.
26 *USNT* General W.G. Haan.
27 General Stuart Heintzelmann *at her fitting-out berth, photograph April 21 1945*

 25

Class P2-S2-R2 (11 Ships)

189.7 × 23.0 m / 622 × 75.5 ft;
Geared turbines, De Laval; 18,700
SHP; Twin screw; 20 kn;
Accommodation for 5,200 troops;
Crew: 476.
Builders: Federal SB & DD Co,
Kearny/NJ.

Turbine steamer *General John Pope*
US Navy

17,833 GRT; Yard no: 268

1943 Mar 21: Launched.
Aug 5: Commissioned. Number:
AP 110.
Sep 5: Maiden voyage Newport-
News-Greenock.
1946 Handed over to the US
Army.
1951 Jul: Placed in MSTS by the
US Navy. Number: T-AP 110.
1958 Sep: To the Maritime
Administration. Laid up at
Olympia.
1965 Aug: Returned to the US
Navy.

Turbine steamer *General A.E. Anderson*
US Navy

17,833 GRT; Yard no: 269

1943 May 2: Launched.
Oct 5: Commissioned. Number:
AP 111.
Oct 25: Maiden voyage Norfolk-
Casablanca.
1949 Oct: Entered MSTS.
Number: T-AP 111.
1958 Laid up by the Maritime
Administration in Suisun Bay.

1/2 The General John Pope *at the building yard shortly before completion (1) and as US Navy transport in 1945.*
3 *USNT* General A.E. Anderson.

1

2

3

Turbine steamer *General W.A. Mann*
US Navy

17,833 GRT; Yard no: 270

1943 Jul 18: Launched.
Oct 13: Commissioned. Number:
AP 112.
Dec: Maiden voyage Norfolk-
North Africa.
1949 Oct: Entered MSTS.
Number: T-AP 112.
1966 Dec 1: Maritime
Administration. Laid up on the
Hudson.

Turbine steamer *General H.W. Butner*
US Navy

17,951; Yard no: 271

1943 Sep 19: Launched.
1944 Jan 11: Commissioned.
Number: AP 113.
Feb 23: Maiden voyage Norfolk-
Morocco.
1949 Oct: Entered MSTS.
Number: T-AP 113.
1960 Mar: Maritime
Administration. Laid up on the
James River.

Turbine steamer *General William Mitchell*
US Navy

17,951 GRT; Yard no: 272

1943 Oct 31: Launched.
1944 Jan 19: Commissioned.
Number: AP 114.
Mar 3: Maiden voyage Norfolk-
Casablanca.
1949 Entered MSTS. Number:
T-AP 114.
1966 Dec 1: Maritime
Administration. Laid up in Suisun
Bay.

4 *The* General W.A. Mann,
photograph November 1943.
5 *USNT* General H.W. Butner.
6 *USNT* General William Mitchell.

4

5

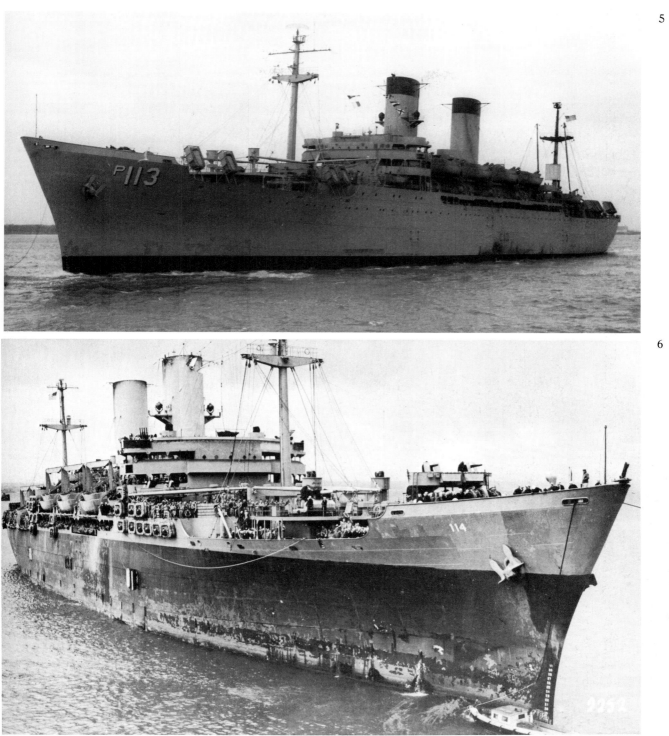

6

Turbine steamer *General George M. Randall*
US Navy

17,833 GRT; Yard no: 273

1944 Jan 30: Launched.
Apr 15: Commissioned. Number: AP 115.
May 23: Maiden voyage Norfolk-Bombay.
1949 Oct: Entered MSTS. Number: T-AP 115.
1962 Maritime Administration. Laid up on the James River.
1975 May 8: Sold to Union Minerals and Alloys Corp, New York, to be broken up.

Turbine steamer *General M.C. Meigs*
US Navy

17,707 GRT; Yard no: 274

1944 Mar 13: Launched.
Jun 3: Commissioned. Number: AP 116.
Jul 10: Maiden voyage Newport News-Naples.
1950 Jul 21: Entered MSTS. Number: T-AP 116.
1958 Oct 1: Maritime Administration. Laid up at Olympia.
1972 Jan: The *General M.C. Meigs* was towed from out of Puget Sound, bound for San Francisco where she was to be laid up again. Jan 9: Off Cape Flattery the towline parted. The ship drifted ashore and broke in two.

Turbine steamer *General W.H. Gordon*
US Navy

17,833 GRT; Yard no: 275

1944 May 7: Launched.
Jun 29: Commissioned. Number: AP 117.
Sep 5: Maiden voyage Boston-Cherbourg.
1946 Jun 18: Chartered to American President Lines. US Army transport.
1951 Nov 8: Entered MSTS. Number: T-AP 117.
1970 Apr 23: Maritime Administration. Laid up at James River.

7 *USNT* General George M. Randall.
8 *USNT* General W.H. Gordon.

7

8

Turbine steamer *General W.P. Richardson*
US Navy

1949 *La Guardia*
1956 *Leilani*
1961 *President Roosevelt*
1970 *Atlantis*
1972 *Emerald Seas*

17,811 GRT; Yard no: 276

1944 Aug 6: Launched. In April 1944 the intended name had been *General R.M. Blatchford.*
Oct 31: Delivered.
Nov 2: Commissioned. Number: AP 118.
Dec 10: Maiden voyage Boston-Southampton.
1946 Feb 14: Handed over to the US Army.
1948 Mar 10: Laid up. Chartered to American Export Lines. Refitted for passenger service at Pascagoula. Renamed *La Guardia.* Passengers: 157 1st class, 452 tourist class.
1949 May 27: First voyage New York-Genoa. From October, to Haifa.
1951 Dec 13: Handed over to the US Maritime Commission. Laid up on the James River.
1955 Sold to Hawaiian SS Co, Textron Inc, New York. 18,298 GRT after refit.
1956 Jul: Renamed *Leilani.* California-Hawaii service.
1958 Textron Inc went bankrupt. Dec 29: The *Leilani* was laid up.
1959 Jun: The Maritime Administration auctioned the ship.
1960 Sold to American President Lines, San Francisco.
1961 Mar 1: Rebuilding as luxury liner commenced by Puget Sound Bridge & DD Co at Seattle. Renamed *President Roosevelt.*

1962 Apr 16: Entered service. 18,920 GRT. 456 1st class passengers.
May 10: First voyage San Francisco-Yokohama.
1970 Sold to D & A Chandris. Registered for Solon Nav SA, Piraeus. Rebuilt at Perama for cruising. Renamed *Atlantis.*
1971 Jun: Completed. 24,458 GRT. 756 passengers in one class, maximum 1092 passengers. Cruising from US ports.
1972 Oct:Sold to Ares Shipping Corp, Panama. Renamed *Emerald Seas.* Again cruising from US ports. 18,936 GRT.

9/10 *The* Leilani *ex* General W.P. Richardson *was sold to American President Lines in 1960 and refitted to become the luxury liner* President Roosevelt.

9

10

Turbine steamer *General William Weigel*
US Navy

17,812 GRT; Yard no: 277

1944 Sep 3: Launched. For a short time in April 1944 the name *General C.H. Barth* had been under consideration.
1945 Jan 6: Commissioned. Number: AP 119.
Feb 11: Maiden voyage New York-Le Havre.
1946 May: Handed over to the US Army.
1951 Aug 1: US Navy. Entered MSTS. Number: T-AP 119.
1958 Jun 12: To the Maritime Administration. Laid up at Olympia.
1965 Aug 18: Returned to service with the US Navy. In MSTM again.
1970 Apr 7: Maritime Administration. Laid up at Suisun.

Turbine steamer *General J.C. Breckinridge*
US Navy

17,811 GRT; Yard no: 505

1945 Mar 18: Launched.
Jun 30: Commissioned. Number: AP 176.
Aug 4: Maiden voyage.
1949 Oct 1: Entered MSTS. Number: T-AP 176.
1966 Dec 1: Maritime Administration. Laid up in Suisun Bay.

11 *The* General William Weigel, *photograph January 1945.*
12 *The* General J.C. Breckinridge, *photograph July 1945.*

11

Class P2-SE2-R1 (8 Ships)

17,100 GRT.
185.6 × 23.0 m / 609 × 75.5 ft;
Turbo-electric drive; Twin screw;
18,000 SHP; 19 kn;
Accommodation for 4,680 troops;
Crew: 367.
Builders: Bethlehem Steel Co,
Alameda/Cal.

Turbo-electric vessel *Admiral W.S. Benson*
US Navy

1947 *Gen. Daniel I. Sultan*

Yard no: 9501

1943 Nov 28: Launched for the US Army.
1944 Aug 23: Delivered to the US Navy. Number: AP 120.
Nov 30: Maiden voyage New Orleans-Bombay.
1946 Jun: US Army.
1947 Renamed *Gen. Daniel I. Sultan.*
1950 Placed in MSTS by the US Navy. Number: T-AP 120.
1968 Nov 7: Maritime Administration. Laid up in reserve fleet.

Turbo-electric vessel *Admiral W.L. Capps*
US Navy

1947 *Gen. Hugh J. Gaffey*

Yard no: 9502

1944 Feb 20: Launched for the US Army.
Sep 18: Delivered to the US Navy. Number: AP 121.
Nov 23: Maiden voyage to the Pacific.
1946 May: Handed over to the US Army.
1947 Renamed *Gen. Hugh J. Gaffey.*
1950 Placed in MSTS by the US Navy. Number: T-AP 121.
1968 Nov 27: Maritime Administration. Laid up.

1 *The* Gen. Daniel I. Sultan *ex* Admiral W.S. Benson, *photograph February 1948.*
2 *The* Gen. Hugh J. Gaffey *ex* Admiral W.L. Capps.

1

2

Turbo-electric vessel *Admiral R.E. Coontz*
US Navy

1947 *Gen. Alexander M. Patch*

Yard no: 9503

1944 Apr 22: Launched for the US Army.
Nov 21: Delivered to the US Navy. Number: AP 122.
1945 Jan 3: Maiden voyage San Francisco-Pearl Harbour.
1946 Mar 25: Handed over to the US Army.
1947 Renamed *Gen. Alexander M. Patch.*
1950 Mar 1: Placed in MSTS by the US Navy. Number: T-AP 122.
1970 May 26: Maritime Administration. Laid up at James River.

Turbo electric vessel *Admiral E.W. Eberle*
US Navy

1947 *Gen. Simon B. Buckner*

Yard no: 9504

1944 Jun 14: Launched for the US Army.
1945 Jan 24: Delivered to the US Navy. Number: AP 123.
Mar 6: Maiden voyage San Francisco-Philippines.
1946 May: Handed over to the US Army.
1947 Renamed *Gen. Simon B. Buckner.*
1950 Mar 1: Placed in MSTS by the US Navy. Number: T-AP 123.
1970 Mar 24: Maritime Administration. Laid up at James River.

3 *The* Gen. Alexander M. Patch *ex* Admiral R.E. Coontz.
4 *The* Gen. Simon B. Buckner *ex* Admiral E.W. Eberle.

3

4

Turbo-electric vessel *Admiral C.F. Hughes*
US Navy

1947 *Gen. Edwin D. Patrick*

Yard no: 9505

1944 Jul 27: Launched for the US Army.
1945 Jan 31:Delivered to the US Navy. Number: AP 124.
Mar 13: Maiden voyage San Francisco-Pearl Harbour.
1946 May: Handed over to the US Army.
1947 Renamed *Gen. Edwin D. Patrick*.
1950 Mar 1: Placed in MSTS by the US Navy. Number: T-AP 124.
1968 Sep 20: Maritime Administration. Laid up in reserve fleet.

Turbo-electric vessel *Admiral H.T. Mayo*
US Navy

1947 *Gen. Nelson M. Walker*

Yard no: 9506

1944 Nov 26: Launched for the US Army.
1945 Apr 24: Delivered to the US Navy. Number: AP 125.
May 24: Maiden voyage San Francisco-Le Havre.
1946 May 27: Handed over to the US Army.
1947 Renamed *Gen. Nelson M. Walker*.
1950 Mar 1: Placed in MSTS by the US Navy. Number: T-AP 125.
1970 Apr 16: Maritime Administration. Laid up at James River.

5/6 *The* Admiral C.F. Hughes, *photograph December 1947* (5), *renamed* Gen. Edwin D. Patrick *by the US Army in 1947.*
7 *The* Gen. Nelson M. Walker *ex* Admiral H.T. Mayo.

5

6

7

Turbo-electric vessel *Admiral Hugh Rodman*
US Navy

1947 *Gen. Maurice Rose*

Yard no: 9507

1945 Feb 25: Launched for the US Army.
Jul 10: Delivered to the US Navy. Number: AP 126.
Aug 21: Maiden voyage.
1946 May: Handed over to the US Army.
1947 Renamed *Gen. Maurice Rose*.
1950 Mar 1: Placed in MSTS by the US Navy. Number: T-AP 126.
1970 Jun 8: Maritime Administration. Laid up at James River.

Turbo-electric vessel *Admiral W.S. Sims*
US Navy

1947 *Gen. William O. Darby*

Yard no: 9508

1945 Jan 4: Launched for the US Army.
Sep 27: Delivered to the US Navy. Number: AP 127.
Oct: Maiden voyage.
1946 Jun: Handed over to the US Army.
1947 Renamed *Gen. William O. Darby*.
1950 Mar 1: Placed in MSTS by US Navy. Number: T-AP 127.
1970 Jun 30: Maritime Administration. Laid up at James River.

8 *The* Admiral Hugh Rodman.
9 *The* Gen. William O. Darby *ex* Admiral W.S. Sims.
10 *Four P2-SE2-R1 ships at Bayonne. From left to right:* Buckner, Darby, Patch *and* Rose.

8

Class C4-S-A3 (15 Ships)

12,420 GRT; 159.3 × 21.7 m / 523 × 71.2 ft; Geared turbines, J. Hendy Iron Works*; Single screw; 9,900 SHP; 17 kn;
Accommodation for 3,800 troops; Crew: 256.
Builders: Kaiser, Vancouver, Wash.**

* The ships *Marine Adder* and *Marine Swallow* had Westinghouse turbines.
**The three ships *Marine Adder*, *Marine Perch* and *Marine Swallow* were built by Kaiser at Richmond, Cal.

This book does not deal with the 15 C4 freighters of the C4-S-B1 and C4-S-B2 classes, which also had *Marine* names and which were completed or rebuilt during the war, some as hospital ships and others as troop transports to carry several hundred.

Turbine steamer *Marine Tiger*
US Maritime Commission, Portland

1966 *Oakland*

Yard no: 501

1945 Mar 23: Launched.
Jul: Completed. Transport service. Managed by Matson Nav Co.
1947 Jun 24: First voyage New York-Le Havre. 850 tourist class passengers.
1949 Sep: Returned to the US Maritime Commission. Laid up.
1966 Sold to Litton Industries Leasing Corp, Wilmington/Del. Rebuilt as container vessel by Ingalls SB Corp. Renamed *Oakland*. 17,184 GRT. Length overall 208.5 × 23.8 m / 684 × 78.1 ft.

Turbine steamer *Marine Shark*
US Maritime Commission, Portland

1968 *Charleston*

Yard no: 502

1945 Apr 4: Launched.
Aug: Completed.
Sep 18: Maiden voyage as a transport under American President Lines management.
1946 May 2: First voyage New York-Naples.
1948 Chartered to United States Lines.
May: First voyage New York-Bremerhaven. 930 tourist class passengers.
1949 Returned to the US Maritime Commission. Laid up.
1967 Sold to Litton Industries Leasing Corp, Wilmington/Del. Rebuilt as a container vessel by Maryland SB & DD Co.
1968 Renamed *Charleston*. 11,389 GRT.

Turbine steamer *Marine Cardinal*
US Maritime Commission, Portland

1967 *Baltimore*
1970 *San Pedro*

Yard no: 503

1945 Apr: Launched.
Sep: Completed.
Sep 27: Maiden voyage in the transport service under American President Lines management. Laid up at the end of the '40s.
1967 Sold to Sea Land Service Inc, Wilmington/Del. Renamed *Baltimore*. Rebuilding as container vessel was carried out by Maryland SB & DD Co. 11,389 GRT.
1970 Refitted at the Todd Shipyard, San Pedro. New container forepart. 18,420 GRT; Length overall 208.5 × 23.8 m / 684 × 78.1 ft. Renamed *San Pedro*.
1974 Sold to Reynolds Leasing Co, Wilmington/Del.

1 *The* Marine Shark.
2 *The* Marine Cardinal, *photograph July 1946.*

1

2

Turbine steamer *Marine Falcon*
US Maritime Commission,
Portland

1966 *Trenton*
1975 *Borinquen*

Yard no: 504

1945 Apr 27: Launched.
Sep: Completed. Maiden voyage in
the transport service.
1947 Apr: Chartered to the United
States Lines for New York-Le
Havre service with 930 tourist class
passengers.
1948 Returned to the US
Maritime Commission. Laid up.
1966 Sold to Litton Industries
Leasing Corp, Wilmington.
Rebuilt by Ingalls at Pascagoula.
New container-midship-section.
17,189 GRT. 208.5 × 23.8 m /
684 × 78.1 ft.
Renamed *Trenton*.
1975 Renamed *Borinquen*.

Turbine steamer *Marine Flasher*
US Maritime Commission,
Portland

1966 *Long Beach*

Yard no: 505

1945 May 16: Launched.
Sep: Completed. Maiden voyage in
the transport service.
1946 Chartered to United States
Lines for New York-Le Havre
service. 914 tourist class
passengers.
May 25: First voyage.
1949 Sep: Returned to the US
Maritime Commission. Laid up.
1966 Sold to Litton Industries
Leasing Corp, Wilmington.
Rebuilt by Ingalls at Pascagoula.
New container-midship-section.
17,814 GRT. 208 × 23.8 m /
684 × 78.1 ft.
Renamed *Long Beach*.
1975 Sold to Reynolds Leasing
Corp.

Turbine steamer *Marine Jumper*
US Maritime Commission,
Portland

1966 *Panama*

Yard no: 506

1945 May 30: Launched.
Oct: Maiden voyage in the
transport service. Matson
management.
1947 Chartered to United States
Lines for New York-Le Havre
service. 850 tourist class
passengers.
Jun 6: First voyage New
York-Gdynia.
1949 Returned to the US
Maritime Commission. Laid up.
1966 Sold to Litton Industries
Leasing Corp, Wilmington.
Rebuilt by Ingalls at Pascagoula.
New container-midship-section.
17,184 GRT. 208.5 × 23.08 m /
684 × 78.1 ft. Renamed *Panama*.

3 *The* Marine Flasher, *photograph
August 1945.*
4 *The* Marine Jumper, *photograph July
1946.*

Turbine steamer *Marine Serpent*
US Maritime Commission,
Portland

1968 *Galveston*

Yard no: 507

1945 Jun 12: Launched.
Sep 21: Delivered.
Oct 31: Maiden voyage in the
transport service. Managed by
United Fruit Co.
1947 Jul: Laid up in Suisun Bay.
1952 May 8: To the US Navy
as a troop transport in the Korean
War. Number: T-AP 202.
1954 Transport service to
Vietnam.
1955 Aug 17: Handed over to
Maritime Administration. Laid up
at Olympia, Puget Sound.
1968 Sold to Sea Land Service Inc,
Portland. Rebuilt as container
vessel by Todd, Los Angeles.
Renamed *Galveston*. 11,389 GRT.
1969 Mar: In service after
rebuilding.

Turbine steamer *Ernie Pyle*
US Maritime Commission,
Portland

1965 *Green Lake*

Yard no: 508

1945 Jun 25: Launched.
Nov 1: Maiden voyage in the
transport service.
1946 Chartered to United States
Lines for New York-Le Havre
service. 869 tourist class
passengers.
Jun 19: First voyage.
1949 Returned to the US
Maritime Commission. Laid up.
1965 Sold to Central Gulf SS Co,
New Orleans. Rebuilt as cargo
vessel by Tampa Ship Repair &
DD Co. Renamed *Green Lake*.
11,021 GRT.

Turbine steamer *Marine Carp*
US Maritime Commission,
Portland

1968 *Green Springs*

Yard no: 509

1945 Jul 5: Launched.
Oct 11: Delivered.
Nov 14: Maiden voyage in the
transport service. Managed by
Matson Nav Co.
1946 Jul 22: First voyage for
American Export Lines, New
York-Piraeus. 900 tourist class
passengers.
1949 US Maritime Commission.
Laid up.
1952 Mar 17: Taken over by the
US Navy because of the Korean
War. Number: T-AP 199.
Served as a troop transport in the
North Atlantic and Far East.
Voyages to US bases in Greenland
and in the Arctic.
1958 Sep 11: Handed over to the
Maritime Administration and laid
up at Beaumont, Texas.
1967 Jul 20: Sold to Central Gulf
SS Co, New Orleans.
Dec: Rebuilding as a cargo vessel
commenced by Tampa Ship
Repair & DD Co.
1968 Jun: Entered service as
Green Springs. 10,575 GRT.

5 *The* Marine Serpent, *photograph
November 1946.*
6 *The* Ernie Pyle.

Turbine steamer *Marine Lynx*
US Maritime Commission,
Portland

1967 *Transcolumbia*

Yard no: 510

1945 Jul 17: Launched.
Oct 22: Delivered.
Dec 3: Maiden voyage in the
transport service. Managed by
Moore-McCormack.
1946 Apr 17: Management
transferred to Matson Nav Co.
1947 Jun 27: One round-the-world
voyage for American President
Lines, then laid up in Suisun Bay.
1950 Jul 23: Commissioned by the
US Navy as a troop transport after
the outbreak of the Korean War.
Number: T-AP 194.
1954 Refugee transport, Vietnam,
then in reserve until 1956.
1956 In service again for Far East
voyages.
1958 May 1: Handed over to the
Maritime Administration and laid
up at Astoria, Oregon.
1967 Aug 4: Sold to Hudson
Waterways Corp, New York.
Rebuilt as a heavy lift carrier by
Savannah Machine & Foundry Co.
Renamed *Transcolumbia*.
1968 Mar: Refit as a car
transporter commenced by SB &
DD Co at Newport News. 10,014
GRT.
1969 Commissioned.

Turbine steamer *Marine Marlin*
US Maritime Commission,
Portland

1965 *Green Bay*

Yard no: 511

1945 Jul 28: Launched.
Nov: Completed.
Dec 5: Maiden voyage in the
transport service.
1946 Chartered to United States
Lines for New York-Le Havre
service. 926 tourist class
passengers.
Sep 16: First voyage.
1949 Returned to Maritime
Commission. Laid up.
1965 Sold to Central Gulf SS
Corp, New Orleans. Rebuilt as a
cargo vessel by Tampa Ship
Repair & DD Co. 11,021 GRT.
Renamed *Green Bay*.
1971 Aug 17: The *Green Bay* sank
in the South Vietnamese port Qui
Nhon after an underwater
explosion which was obviously the
work of the Vietcong.
Aug 31: The ship was raised, and,
considered not worth repairing.
Sold to the Leung Yau
Shipbreaking Co, Hong Kong.
Oct 1: Arrived at Hong Kong after
voyage in tow.

Turbine steamer *Marine Phoenix*
US Maritime Commission,
Portland

1967 *Mohawk*

Yard no: 512

1945 Aug 9: Launched.
Nov 9: Delivered.
Dec 12: Maiden voyage Seattle-
Nagoya under Moore-McCormack
management.
1947 Laid up in Suisun Bay.
1950 Jul 21: Commissioned by the
US Navy after the outbreak of the
Korean War. Number: T-AP 195.
1958 Nov 3: Laid up on the
Columbia River.
1967 Apr 25: Sold to Mohawk
Shipping Inc, New York.
Rebuilding as a cargo vessel
commenced in May by Jacksonville
Shipyard.
Renamed *Mohawk*. 10,625 GRT.
1968 Apr: Commissioned.

7 *The* Marine Lynx.

Turbine steamer *Marine Adder*
US Maritime Commission,
San Francisco

1967 *Transcolorado*

Yard no: 46

1945 May 16: Launched.
Oct 5:Delivered.
Nov: Maiden voyage in the
transport service to the Far East.
Managed by American President
Lines.
1947 Laid up in Suisun Bay.
1950 Jul 24: Commissioned by the
US Navy. Number: T-AP 193.
Troop transport in the Korean
War. Served for Vietnam also after
1954.
1957 Jun 6: Maritime
Administration. Laid up at
Astoria, Oregon.
1967 Aug 4: Sold to Hudson
Waterways Corp, New York.
Rebuilt as a cargo vessel by
Savannah Machine & Foundry Co.
Renamed *Transcolorado*.
1968 Mar: Refitted as a car
transporter by Newport News SB &
DD Co. 10,014 GRT.

Turbine steamer *Marine Perch*
US Maritime Commission,
San Francisco

1965 *Yellowstone*

Yard no: 47

1945 Jun 25: Launched.
Oct: Completed.
1946 New York-Europe service
under charter to United States
Lines. 901 tourist class passengers.
Apr 29: First voyage in American-
Scantic service, New York-
Gothenburg.
Sep 26: First voyage New York-
Naples for American Export Lines.
1948 Returned to Maritime
Commission. Laid up.
1965 Sold to Rio Grande
Transport Inc, New York. Rebuilt
as a bulk carrier by Tampa Ship
Repair & DD Co.
Renamed *Yellowstone*. 11,034
GRT.

Turbine steamer *Marine Swallow*
US Maritime Commission,
San Francisco

1965 *Missouri*
1974 *Ogden Missouri*

Yard no: 48

1945 Jun 21: Launched.
Nov: Completed.
Dec 23: Maiden voyage in the
transport service. Managed by
American President Lines.
1947 Laid up.
1948 Jul 26: first voyage New
York-Bremerhaven for United
States Lines. Laid up again after
two round voyages.
1965 Sold to Meadowbrook
Transport Inc, New York.
Jan: Rebuilding commenced as
bulk carrier by Tampa Ship Repair
& DD Co.
Renamed *Missouri*. 11,034 GRT.
Managed by Oriental Exporters
Inc.
1974 To Ogden Missouri
Transport Inc, Panama, as *Ogden
Missouri*.

8 *The* Marine Adder, *photograph
November 1946.*
9 *The* Marine Swallow, *photograph
July 1946.*

La Marseillaise

Motorship *La Marseillaise*
Messageries Maritimes, Marseille

Launched as *Maréchal Pétain*
1957 *Arosa Sky*
1958 *Bianca C.*

Builders: Constructions Navales,
La Ciotat
Yard no: 161
17,321 GRT; 180.8 × 23.0 m /
593 × 75.5 ft; Sulzer diesels, Cie
de Const Méc; Triple screw;
31,500 BHP; 20, max 22 kn;
Passengers: 344 1st class, 74 2nd
class, 318 3rd class.

1939 Laid down.
1944 Launched as *Maréchal
Pétain.* The hull was subsequently
towed to Port Bouc.
Aug: The Germans sank the
incomplete ship during their
retreat from Southern France.
1946 Having been renamed *La
Marseillaise* in the meantime, the
ship was raised and towed to
Toulon, and later to the builders
yard at La Ciotat.
1949 Jul: Completed.
Aug 18: Maiden voyage Marseille-
Yokohama.
1957 Sold to Arosa Line Inc,
Panama.
Renamed *Arosa Sky.*
Refit of passenger
accommodation: 202 1st class,
1,030 tourist class.
May 10: First voyage
Bremerhaven-New York.
1958 In October, the Arosa Line,
which was threatened with
bankruptcy, sold their flagship to
G. Costa du Andrea, Genoa.
Renamed *Bianca C.*
1959 After modernisation of the
passenger accommodation, the
ship entered the Naples-Genoa-
La Guaira service. 18,427 GRT.

1961 Oct 22: While anchored off
St George, Grenada, the *Bianca C.*
caught fire after an explosion in
the engine room. The flames soon
spread to every deck and the ship
had to be abandoned. All 673
people on board, with the
exception of one crew member who
was never found, were brought to
safety in the ship's boats and in
craft which had hurried out from
the shore. Two badly injured
people died later from their burns.
Oct 24: The British frigate
Londonderry succeeded in
securing a towing cable on the still
burning wreck.
The attempt, however, to beach
the *Bianca C.* failed because the
burnt-out hull sprang a leak and
sank in deep water.

1/2 *Launched as the* Maréchal Pétain
in 1944, La Marseillaise *(1) was sold to
the Arosa Line in 1957 and renamed*
Arosa Sky *(2).*

1

2

Naviera Aznar Monte Ships

Motorship *Monte Urbasa*
Naviera Aznar, Bilbao

Launched as *Escorial*
1969 *Cabo Santa Paula*

Builders: Soc Espanola de
Construction Naval, Bilbao
Yard no: 55
10,142 GRT; 148.5 × 19.0 m /
487 × 62.3 ft; Sulzer diesels;
Single screw; 7,300 BHP; 16 kn;
Passengers: 4 1st class, 58 tourist
class, 328 3rd class.

1945 Sep 7: Launched as cargo
vessel *Escorial* for the Spanish
state owned Empresa Nacional
'Elcano', Bilbao.
1947 Sold to Naviera Aznar.
Building continued to revised
plans for a cargo and passenger
vessel.
1948 Apr: Completed as *Monte
Urbasa*. Measurement as a shelter
decker. 7,723 GRT.
Entered Genoa-Central America
service.
1969 Sold to Ybarra y Cia, Seville.
Passenger accommodation
removed. Shelter deck
measurement 6,714 GRT.
Renamed *Cabo Santa Paula*.
Genoa-Buenos Aires service.

Motorship *Monte Udala*
Naviera Aznar, Bilbao

Builders: Cia Euskalduna, Bilbao
Yard no: 133
10,170 GRT; 148.5 × 19.0 m /
487 × 62.3 ft; Sulzer diesels;
Single screw; 7,300 BHP; 16, max
17 kn; Passengers: 62 1st class, 40
2nd class, 290 3rd class.

1946 May 1: Launched. The keel
had been laid down as a cargo
vessel of the Monasterio-class for
Empresa Nacional 'Elcano'.
1948 Jul: Completed.
Genoa-Buenos Aires service.
1971 Sep 8: During a voyage from
Buenos Aires to Genoa the *Monte
Udala* sprang a leak in the engine
room and had to be abandoned in
a sinking condition. The ship sank
70 nautical miles off Ilheus in
position 15° 02′S-36° 38′W.

1 *The* Monte Urbasa *has been sailing
purely as a cargo vessel since 1969.*
2 *The sister ship* Monte Udala *sank off
South America in 1971.*

The Modjokerto

Motorship *Modjokerto*
Rotterdam Lloyd, Rotterdam

1963 *Dona Rita*
1968 *Atlas Promoter*

Builders: Caledon, Dundee
Yard no: 422
10,116 GRT; 151.6 × 19.6 m /
497 × 64.3 ft; Burmeister & Wain
diesels, Kincaid; Single screw;
7,500 BHP; 15 kn; Passengers: 36
in one class.

1946 Launched. She had been laid
down as a fast standard cargo
vessel for the British Ministry of
War Transport.
Dec: Completed. The *Modjokerto*
was used by her owners principally
between European ports and the
Far East.
1963 Sold to Socrates Nav Co Ltd,
Monrovia. 10,014 GRT.
Renamed *Dona Rita*.
1968 Sold to Korea Atlas Line,
Inchon.
Renamed *Atlas Promoter*.
1970 9,857 GRT.
1972 Sep 23: Arrived at
Kaohsiung. Broken up by Tai Kien
Industry Co Ltd.

1 *Rotterdam Lloyd's* Modjokerto.

1

Steamship *Lancashire*
Bibby Line, Liverpool

Builders: Harland & Wolff,
Belfast
Yard no: 459
10,391 GRT; 153.0 × 17.4 m /
501 × 57.1 ft; IV exp eng,
H & W; Twin screw; 6,500 IHP;
15 kn; Passengers:
approximately 1,000 troops; Crew:
200.

1917 Jan 11: Launched.
Jul: Completed as a passenger and
cargo ship. 295 passengers in one
class. 9,445 GRT. Liverpool-
Rangoon service, under
government control until 1918.
1918 Troop and repatriation
transport until 1920.
1920 Re-entered Liverpool-
Rangoon service after conversion
to oil-firing by Harland & Wolff.
1930 Rebuilt as a full-time troop
transport by Cammell Laird at
Birkenhead.
Served in India-Far East.
1946 Jul: To Glasgow for
accommodation modernisation.
Re-entered service at end of year.
10,331 GRT.
1956 Apr 6: Arrived at Barrow.
Broken up by T.W. Ward.

1

1 *The Bibby Liner* Lancashire *sailed
from 1930 as a full-time troop
transport.*

Delta Liners

Turbine steamer *Del Norte*
Delta SS Lines Inc, New Orleans

Builders: Ingalls, Pascagoula
Yard no: 437
10,073 GRT; 150.6 × 21.1 m /
494 × 69.2 ft; Geared turbines,
General Electric Co; Single screw;
8,750 SHP; 17 kn; Passengers: 120
1st class.

1946 Jan 11: Launched.
Following completion at the end of
1948, she went into the Mississipi
Shipping Company's New Orleans-
Buenos Aires service.
1969 8,638 GRT.
1972 Feb 12: Arrived at
Kaohsiung to be broken up.

Turbine steamer *Del Sud*
Delta SS Lines Inc, New Orleans

Builders: Ingalls, Pascagoula
Yard no: 438
10,073 GRT; 150.6 × 21.1 m /
494 × 69.2 ft; Geared turbines,
General Electric Co; Single screw;
9,350 SHP; 17, max 18 kn;
Passengers: 120 1st class.

1946 Feb 22: Launched.
1947 Completed. Entered
Mississippi Shipping Co's New
Orleans-Buenos Aires service.
1969 8,638 GRT.
1972 Sold to be broken up.

Turbine steamer *Del Mar*
Delta SS Lines Inc, New Orleans

Builders: Ingalls, Pascagoula
Yard no: 439
10,073 GRT; 150.6 × 21.1 m /
494 × 69.2 ft; Geared turbines,
General Electric Co; Single screw;
9,350 SHP; 17, max 18 kn;
Passengers: 120 1st class.

1946 May 17: Launched.
1947 Completed. Entered
Mississippi Shipping Co's New
Orleans-Buenos Aires service.
1969 8,638 GRT.
1972 Feb 16: Arrived at
Kaohsiung to be broken up.

1/2 *The three sister ships* Del Norte
(*1*), Del Sud *and* Del Mar (*2*) *served
the New Orleans-Buenos Aires route
until 1972.*

The Corinthic Class

Turbine steamer *Corinthic*
Shaw, Savill & Albion,
Southampton

·Builders: Cammell Laird,
Birkenhead
Yard no: 1175
15,682 GRT; 170.6 × 21.7 m /
560 × 71.2 ft; Geared turbines
from builders; Twin screw; 14,000
SHP; 17 kn; Passengers: 85 1st
class.

1946 May 30: Launched.
1947 Apr: Completed.
Apr 12: Maiden voyage Liverpool-
Sydney. Then entered London-
New Zealand service.
1965 Passenger accommodation
removed at Schiedam.
Measurement as cargo vessel:
14,285 GRT.
1969 Oct 23: Arrived at
Kaohsiung to be broken up.

Turbine steamer *Athenic*
Shaw Savill & Albion,
Southampton

Builders: Harland & Wolff,
Belfast
Yard no: 1326
15,187 GRT; 171.8 × 21.7 m /
564 × 71.2 ft; Geared turbines,
H & W; Twin screw; 14,000 SHP;
17 kn; Passengers: 85 1st class.

1946 Nov 26: Launched.
1947 Jul: Completed.
Aug 1: Maiden voyage London-
New Zealand.
1965 Passenger accommodation
removed at Newcastle. Now 14,248
GRT.
1969 Oct 25: Arrived at
Kaohsiung to be broken up.

1/2 *The* Corinthic (*1*) *and her sister
ship* Athenic (*2*), *were built for the
Australia service.*

Turbine steamer *Gothic*
Shaw, Savill & Albion,
Southampton

Builders: Swan, Hunter &
Wigham Richardson, Newcastle
Yard no: 1759
15,902 GRT; 171.0 × 22.0 m /
561 × 72.2 ft; Geared turbines
from builders; Twin screw; 14,000
SHP; 17 kn; Passengers: 85 1st
class.

1947 Dec 12: Launched.
1948 Dec: Completed.
Dec 23: Maiden voyage Liverpool-
Sydney. Then entered
London-New Zealand service.
1951 Refitted by Cammell Laird
for service as a royal yacht for the
planned visit of the British Royal
Family to Australia and New
Zealand which did not take place
because of the death of King
George VI.

1953 Sep/Oct: Fitted out again as
royal yacht for Queen Elizabeth's
visit to Australia and New
Zealand. Funnel lengthened by
about seven feet.
1968 Aug 2: During a voyage from
Wellington to Liverpool a fire in
the liner's superstructure claimed
seven lives. The *Gothic* returned to
Wellington, where the
structural damage was temporarily
repaired. 15,109 GRT.
On October 10 the ship arrived at
Liverpool. The fire damage was
never completely made good, and
after one more round voyage to
New Zealand the liner was sold to
be broken up.
1969 Aug 13: Arrived at
Kaohsiung. The *Gothic* made her
last voyage as a unit of the fleet of
the Cairn Line, also a constituent
of the Furness group.

Turbine steamer *Ceramic*
Shaw, Savill & Albion,
Southampton

Builders: Cammell Laird,
Birkenhead
Yard no: 1185
15,896 GRT; 171.9 × 22.0 m /
564 × 72.2 ft; Geared turbines
from builders; Twin screw; 14,000
SHP; 17 kn; Passengers: 85 1st
class.

1947 Dec 30: Launched.
1948 Oct: Completed.
Nov 16: Maiden voyage Liverpool-
New Zealand, then London-New
Zealand service.
1972 Jun 13: Arrived at Antwerp.
Broken up by Boel & Fils at
Tamise.

3

3/4 *The* Gothic *(3) was fitted out as a royal yacht (4) for Queen Elizabeth's visit to Australia in 1953.*
5 *The last ship of the class, the* Ceramic.

Turbo-electric vessel *President Cleveland*
American President Lines, San Francisco

1973 *Oriental President*

Builders: Bethlehem Alameda Shipyard
Yard no: 9509
15,359 GRT; 185.6 × 23.0 m / 609 × 75.5 ft; Turbo-electric machinery from General Electric Co; 20,000 SHP; 19 kn; Passengers: 324 1st class, 454 tourist class; Crew: 340.

1946 Jun 23: Launched.
1947 Nov: Completed.
Dec 15: Maiden voyage San Francisco-Hong Kong.
1960 Modernisation of passenger accommodation. 14,456 GRT.
1973 Jan: Laid up. Sold to C.Y. Tung group, Hong Kong. Registered under the ownership of Oceanic Cruises Development Inc. Renamed *Oriental President*.
1974 Jun: Arrived at Kaohsiung to be broken up.

Turbo-electric vessel *President Wilson*
American President Lines, San Francisco

1973 *Oriental Empress*

Builders: Bethlehem Alameda Shipyard
Yard no: 9510
15,359 GRT; 185.6 × 23.0 m / 609 × 75.5 ft; Turbo-electric machinery from General Electric Co; 20,000 SHP; 19 kn; Passengers: 324 1st class, 454 tourist class; Crew: 340.

1946 Nov 24: Launched.
1948 Apr: Completed.
Apr 27: Maiden voyage San Francisco-Hong Kong.
1960 Modernisation of passenger accommodation. 15,446 GRT.
1973 Jan: Sold to the Tung group in Hong Kong. Delivered in April. Registered under the ownership of Transocean Lines Ltd, Panama. Renamed *Oriental Empress*. Remained in transpacific service.
1974 Jan: Laid up at Hong Kong.
Jul: Some voyages in Far Eastern waters.
1975 Sep 11: Laid up at Hong Kong.

1/2 *The sister ships* President Cleveland (*1*) *and* President Wilson (*2*) *were developments of the troop transport class P2.*

1

2

The Willem Ruys

Motorship *Willem Ruys*
Rotterdamsche Lloyd, Rotterdam

1965 *Achille Lauro*

Builders: 'De Schelde', Vlissingen
Yard no: 214
21,119 GRT; 192.4 × 25.1 m /
631 × 82.3 ft; Sulzer geared
diesels, six of the eight engines
from 'De Schelde', two from
Sulzer; Twin screw; 38,000 BHP;
22, max 24.62 kn; Passengers:
900.

1939 Jan: Laid down.
1940 Hardly any work was done
on the ship during the German
occupation of the Netherlands.
Any building progress made was
reversed by the activities of
resistance groups.
1946 Jul 1: Launched.
1947 Nov 21: Delivered.

Dec 2: Maiden voyage Rotterdam-
Indonesia.
1957 Dec: Passenger service to
Indonesia ceased.
1958 May: First voyage
Rotterdam-New York. After two
Montreal voyages for Europa-
Canada Line the *Willem Ruys* was
rebuilt by Wilton-Fijenoord for the
round-the-world service.
1959 Mar 7: Entered service after
rebuilding work. 23,114 GRT.
Passengers: 275 1st class, 770
tourist class. Route: Rotterdam-
Suez-Australia-New Zealand-
Panama-Rotterdam.
1964 Jan: Sold to Achille Lauro,
delivered in December.
1965 Jan: Handed over to Flotta
Lauro, Rome.
Renamed *Achille Lauro*.
Rebuilt and modernised by
CN Riuniti di Palermo.

Aug 29: Work considerably
delayed by an explosion and
resulting fire.
1966 Apr 13: First voyage Genoa-
Sydney-Wellington. 23,629 GRT.
Passengers: 152 1st class, 1,155
tourist class.
1972 May 19: Badly damaged by
fire during overhaul work at
Genoa. In service again after five
months.
1972 Dec: Service to Australia
ended. Cruising only.
1975 Apr 28: Collided in the
Dardanelles with the Lebanese
cattle transporter *Yousset,* which
immediately sank. One dead.

1 *The original appearance of the*
Willem Ruys.
2 *In 1959 the* Willem Ruys *was rebuilt*
for the round-the-world service.
3 *The* Achille Lauro *ex* Willem Ruys.

2

3

The Motorship Stockholm

Motorship *Stockholm*
Swedish-America Line,
Gothenburg

1960 *Völkerfreundschaft*

Builders: Götaverken, Gothenburg
Yard no: 611
11,700 GRT; 160.1 × 21.0 m /
525 × 68.9 ft; Götaverken diesels;
Twin screw; 12,000 BHP; 19, max
20 kn; Passengers: 113 1st class,
282 tourist class; Crew: 220.

1946 Sep 9: Launched.
1948 Feb: Completed.
Feb 21: Maiden voyage
Gothenburg-New York. Also
cruising.
1952 12,644 GRT after refit.
Passengers: 86 (from 1955, 24) 1st
class, 584 tourist class.
1956 Jul 25: The *Stockholm*
collided with the Italian Liner
Andrea Doria in thick fog 100
nautical miles off New York. The
Andrea Doria sank several hours
later with 47 dead. The badly
damaged *Stockholm*, aboard
which five people had died in the
collision, reached New York under
her own steam.
Repair work lasting until
November 5 was carried out by the
Bethlehem Steel Co. The
Stockholm was given an entirely
new forepart.
1960 Jan 3: The Free German
Trade Unions Confederation of
East Germany bought the ship and
renamed her *Völkerfreundschaft*.
The VEB Deutsche Seereederei,
Rostock, took over the
management of the ship, which
was used for cruising. 12,442
GRT. 568 passengers in one class.
1972 12,068 GRT.

1/2 *The first post-war new ship of the
Swedish-America Line was sold to
Rostock in 1960 and renamed*
Völkerfreundschaft.

Blue Star Liners

Turbine steamer *Argentina Star*
Blue Star Line, London

Builders: Cammell Laird,
Birkenhead
Yard no: 1173
10,716 GRT; 153.3 × 20.8 m /
503 × 68.2 ft; Parsons geared
turbines from builders; Single
screw; 8,700 SHP; 16 kn;
Passengers: 51 1st class.

1946 Sep 26: Launched.
1947 Jun: Completed.
Jun 14: Maiden voyage London-
Buenos Aires.
1970 10,498 GRT.
1972 Oct 19: Arrived at
Kaohsiung to be broken up by Hi
Yo Steel & Iron Works.

Turbine steamer *Brasil Star*
Blue Star Line, London

Builders: Cammell Laird,
Birkenhead
Yard no: 1174
10,716 GRT; 153.3 × 20.8 m /
503 × 68.2 ft; Parsons geared
turbines from builders; Single
screw; 8,700 SHP; 16 kn;
Passengers: 53 1st class.

1947 Mar 6: Launched.
Oct: Completed.
London-Buenos Aires service.
1970 10,499 GRT.
1972 Oct 10: Arrived at
Kaohsiung to be broken up by
Tung Seng Steel & Iron Works.

1/2 *The* Argentina Star *(1) and* Brasil
Star *(2), built in 1946 and 1947
respectively for the London-South
America service.*

Turbine steamer *Uruguay Star*
Blue Star Line, London

Builders: Cammell Laird,
Birkenhead
Yard no: 1180
10,723 GRT; 153.3 × 20.8 m /
503 × 68.2 ft; Parsons geared
turbines from builders; Single
screw; 8,700 SHP; 16 kn;
Passengers: 53 1st class.

1947 Oct 15: Launched.
1948 May: Completed.
May 22: Maiden voyage from
Liverpool. Thereafter
London-Buenos Aires service.
1970 10,506 GRT.
1972 Aug 25: Arrived at
Kaohsiung to be broken up by Nan
Feng Steel Enterprise Co.

Turbine steamer *Paraguay Star*
Blue Star Line, London

Builders: Cammell Laird,
Birkenhead
Yard no: 1181
10,722 GRT; 153.3 × 20.8 m /
503 × 68.2 ft; Parsons geared
turbines from builders; Single
screw; 8,700 SHP; 16 kn;
Passengers: 53 1st class.

1948 Apr 23: Launched.
Oct: Completed.
London-Buenos Aires service.
1969 Aug 12: While at London
badly damaged by a fire in the
engine room and in the adjacent
refrigeration chambers.
Sep 19: Arrived at Hamburg to be
broken up by Eckardt & Co.

3/4 *The Blue Star Liners* Uruguay Star
and Paraguay Star.

Kampala and Karanja

Turbine steamer *Kampala*
British India Line, London

Builders: Stephen, Glasgow
Yard no: 611
10,304 GRT; 154.5 × 20.2 m /
507 × 66.3 ft; Parsons geared
turbines, Stephen; Twin screw;
9,700 SHP; 16 kn; Passengers: 60
1st class, 180 2nd class, 800 3rd
class.

1946 Dec 10: Launched.
1947 Aug: Completed.
Bombay-Durban service.
1971 Jul 24: Arrived at Kaohsiung
to be broken up by China Steel Co.

Turbine steamer *Karanja*
British India Line, London

Builders: Stephen, Glasgow
Yard no: 616
10,294 GRT; 154.5 × 20.2 m /
507 × 66.3 ft; Parsons geared
turbines, Stephen; Twin screw;
9,700 SHP; 16 kn; Passengers: 60
1st class, 180 2nd class, 800 3rd
class.

1948 Mar 10: Launched.
Oct: Completed. Bombay-Durban
service.
1976 Jun 9: Laid up at Bombay.

1/2 *The British India Line placed the
sister ships* Kampala (*1*) *and* Karanja
(*2*) *in service on the Bombay-Durban
route in 1947.*
3 *During the '50s the ships' hulls were
painted white. The photograph shows
the* Karanja.

1

Three Cunard Liners

Turbine steamer *Media*
Cunard-White Star Line,
Liverpool

1961 *Flavia*

Builders: Brown, Clydebank
Yard no: 629
13,345 GRT; 162.0 × 21.3 m /
531 × 69.9 ft; Geared turbines,
Brown; Twin screw; 15,000 SHP;
18 kn; Passengers: 250 1st class;
Crew: 184.

1946 Dec 12: Launched.
1947 Aug: Completed.
Aug 20: Maiden voyage Liverpool-
New York.
1961 Oct: Sold to Cogedar Line,
Genoa. Renamed *Flavia*.
Rebuilt and modernised by
Officine A & R Navi, Genoa,
work lasting until 1962. 15,465
GRT. 169.8 m / 557 ft length
overall. 1,224 passengers in one
class.
1962 Sep: First voyage Genoa-
Sydney.
Dec: Bremerhaven-Sydney service.
1963 Rotterdam-Panama-New
Zealand-Australia-Mediterranean-
Rotterdam service.
1968 Cruising.
1969 Sold to Costa Armatori,
Genoa. Cruising from Miami.

1/2 The Media, *Cunard Line's first
post-war ship (1), was sold to Italy in
1961 to become the* Flavia *(2).*

1

2

Turbine steamer *Parthia*
Cunard-White Star Line,
Liverpool

1962 *Remuera*
1964 *Aramac*

Builders: Harland & Wolff,
Belfast
Yard no: 1331
13,362 GRT; 162.1 × 21.3 m /
532 × 69.9 ft; Geared turbines,
H & W; Twin screw; 15,000 SHP;
18 kn; Passengers: 251 1st class;
Crew: 184.

1947 Feb 25: Launched.
1948 Apr: Completed.
Apr 10: Maiden voyage Liverpool-
New York.
1961 Nov 1: Sold to the New
Zealand Shipping Company,
London. Passenger
accommodation refitted by
Stephen, Glasgow.
1962 Jun 1: First voyage London-
Wellington. 13,619 GRT. 350
passengers in one class. Renamed
Remuera.
1964 Sold to Eastern & Australian
SS Co, London. Renamed
Aramac.
1965 Feb 8: First voyage
Melbourne-Yokohama.
1967/68 For some time registered
under the ownership of the Federal
SN Co.
1969 Nov 22: Arrived at
Kaohsiung to be broken up.

3/4 The Parthia *became the* Remuera
(3) in 1962. In 1964 she was renamed
Aramac *(4).*

Turbine steamer *Caronia*
Cunard-White Star Line,
Liverpool

1968 *Columbia*
1968 *Caribia*

Builders: Brown, Clydebank
Yard no: 635
34,183 GRT; 217.9 × 27.8 m /
715 × 91.5 ft; Geared turbines,
Brown; Twin screw; 35,000 SHP;
22 kn; Passengers: 581 1st class,
351 cabin class; Crew: 600.

1947 Oct 30: Launched.
1948 Dec: Completed.
1949 Jan 4: Maiden voyage
Southampton-New York. Also
cruising.
1956 34,172 GRT. Passengers:
500 1st class, 330 tourist class.
1965 Oct: Modernisation of
passenger accommodation, the
work lasting until December.
34,274 GRT.
1968 A plan to sell the ship to the
Yugoslavian company Domus-
Turist, which wanted to use the
ship as a floating hotel, at
Dubrovnik or some other Yugoslav
port, fell through.
May: Sold to Universal Line, SA,
Panama.
Jul 26: Handed over to the new
owners and renamed *Columbia*.
Renamed *Caribia* at the end of the
year after a refit at Piraeus. 25,794
GRT. Cruising.
1969 Mar 11: One man was killed
in an explosion in the engine room
during a West Indies cruise. The
ship subsequently drifted for a
day, unmanoeuverable, until she
could be brought in to St Thomas.
Mar 25: Arrived at New York.
Laid up.
1974 Jan: Sold to Taiwan
breakers.

Apr 27: Left New York for
Kaohsiung in tow of German tug
Hamburg.
Aug 12: The *Hamburg* had to put
in to Guam in very heavy weather
for repairs to one of her generators.
The storm forced the tug and the
Caribia towards the harbour. At
the entrance to Apra harbour the
liner struck the breakwater, heeled
over and broke into three sections,
the bow section blocking the
harbour entrance for some time.

5/6 Painted in shades of green, the
Caronia's *colour scheme differed from
that practised by Cunard hitherto.
Picture 6 shows the* Caronia *after her
1965 refit.*

5

6

Elder Dempster Liners

Motorship *Accra*
Elder Dempster Lines, Liverpool

Builders: Vickers Armstrongs,
Barrow
Yard no: 948
11,599 GRT; 143.6 × 20.2 m /
471 × 66.3 ft; Doxford diesels
from builders; Twin screw; 9,400
BHP; 15.5 kn; Passengers: 259 1st
class, 24 3rd class.

1947 Feb 24: Launched.
Sep: Completed.
Liverpool-Apapa service.
1959 11,644 GRT.
1967 Nov 13: Arrived at
Cartagena to be broken up.

Motorship *Apapa*
Elder Dempster Lines, Liverpool

1968 Taipooshan

Builders: Vickers Armstrongs,
Barrow
Yard no: 949
11,607 GRT; 143.6 × 20.2 m /
471 × 66.3 ft; Doxford diesels
from builders; Twin screw; 9,400
BHP; 15.5 kn; Passengers: 259 1st
class, 24 2nd class.

1947 Sep 1: Launched.
1948 Mar: Completed.
Mar 11: Maiden voyage Liverpool-
Apapa service.
1960 11,651 GRT.
1968 Sold to Shun Cheong SN Co,
Liverpool. Renamed *Taipooshan*.

Hong Kong-Penang service.
1975 Feb 28: Breaking up
commenced at Kaohsiung by Fu
Chiang Steel & Iron Co.

1 *The* Accra *entered service in 1947.*
2/3 *The* Apapa *sailed on the Liverpool-
Apapa route until 1968, and was then
sold for Far East service to become the*
Taipooshan.

1

2

3

Turbine steamer *Patria*
Cia Colonial, Lisbon

Builders: Brown, Clydebank
Yard no: 641
13,196 GRT; 162.0 × 20.8 m /
531 × 68.2 ft; Parsons geared
turbines, Brown; Twin screw;
15,000 SHP; 17 kn; Passengers:
114 1st class, 156 tourist class, 320
3rd class; Crew: 193.

1947 Jun 30: Launched.
Dec: Completed.
1948 Jan: Maiden voyage Lisbon-
Cape Town-Mozambique.
1973 Aug 1: Arrived at Kaohsiung
to be broken up.

Turbine steamer *Império*
Cia Colonial, Lisbon

Builders: Brown, Clydebank
Yard no: 642
13,186 GRT; 162.0 × 20.8 m /
531 × 68.2 ft; Parsons geared
turbines, Brown; Twin screw;
15,000 SHP; 17 kn; Passengers:
114 1st class, 156 tourist class, 320
3rd class; Crew: 193.

1947 Dec 27: Launched.
1948 Jun: Completed.
Lisbon-Cape Town-Mozambique
service.
1974 Mar 29: Arrived at
Kaohsiung to be broken up by Chi
Shun Hwa Steel & Iron Co Ltd.

1/2 *Cia Colonial had the sister ships*
Patria *(1) and* Império *(2) built for the*
Africa service in 1947/48.

Motorship *Angola*
Cia Nacional, Lisbon

Builders: Hawthorn Leslie,
Newcastle
Yard no: 689
12,975 GRT; 167.5 × 20.5 m /
550 × 67.3 ft; Doxford diesels
from builders; Twin screw; 15,000
BHP; 17 kn; Passengers: 89 1st
class, 141 tourist class, 98 3rd
class, 413 steerage.

1948 Mar 24: Launched.
Dec: Completed.
1949 Jan: Maiden voyage Lisbon-
Cape Town-Nacala.
1962 13,078 GRT.
1974 Feb 8: Arrived at Chou's
Iron & Steel Co, Hualien, to be
broken up.

Motorship *Moçambique*
Cia Nacional, Lisbon

Builders: Swan, Hunter &
Wigham Richardson, Newcastle
Yard no: 1856
12,976 GRT; 167.5 × 20.5 m /
550 × 67.3 ft; Doxford diesels
from builders; Twin screw; 15,000
BHP; 17 kn; Passengers: 95 1st
class, 141 tourist class, 102 3rd
class, 413 steerage.

1948 Dec 1: Launched.
1949 Oct: Completed.
Lisbon-Cape Town-Nacala service.
1972 Sep 29: Arrived at
Kaohsiung to be broken up.

3/4 *The Cia Nacional placed the two
passenger ships* Angola (*3*) *and*
Moçambique (*4*) *on their Africa
service.*

3

Motorship *Albertville*
Compagnie Maritime Belge,
Antwerp

Builders: Cockerill, Hoboken
Yard no: 717
10,901 GRT; 153.7 × 19.6 m /
504 × 69.3 ft; Burmeister & Wain
diesels, Cockerill; Single screw;
7,200 BHP; 15.5 kn; Later 9,250
BHP and 16.5 kn after exhaust gas
turbocharging of the engines;
Passengers: 207 in one class; Crew:
100.

1947 Jul 1: Launched.
1948 May 8: Completed.
May 17: Delivered.
Jun 12: Maiden voyage Antwerp-
Matadi.
1966 10,576 GRT. 1970 10,528
GRT.
1973 Apr 19: Arrived at
Kaohsiung to be broken up by Nan
Feng Steel Enterprises.

Motorship *Leopoldville*
Compagnie Maritime Belge,
Antwerp

1967 *P.E. Lumumba*

Builders: Cockerill, Hoboken
Yard no: 718
10,901 GRT; 153.7 × 19.6 m/
504 × 69.3 ft; Burmeister & Wain
diesels, Cockerill; Single screw;
7,200 BHP; 15.5 kn; Passengers:
207 in one class; Crew: 137.

1947 Oct 25: Launched.
1948 Sep 3/6: Trials.
Sep 6: Delivered.
Sep: Maiden voyage
Antwerp-Matadi.
1957 Feb 26: Trials after engine
refit. 9,250 BHP and 16.5 knots
after turbocharging.
1967 Sold to Cie Mar Congolaise,
Matadi. Renamed *P.E.
Lumumba.* Continued in same
service. 10,576 GRT.
1972 The owners started to
operate as Cie Mar du Zaire.
1973 May 3: Arrived at Tamise to
be broken up by Boel.
1974 Feb: Sold again to van
Heyghen Frères, Ghent. Partly
broken up.
Aug: Towed to Rio Grande, and
broken up there by Siderurgica
Riograndese SA.

1 *The* Albertville *entered service in
1948, the first of five sister ships.*
2 *In 1967 the* Leopoldville *became the*
P.E. Lumumba.

1

2

Motorship *Elisabethville*
Compagnie Maritime Belge,
Antwerp

Builders: Cockerill, Hoboken
Yard no: 719
10,901 GRT; 153.7 × 19.6 m /
504 × 64.3 ft; Burmeister & Wain
diesels, Cockerill; Single screw;
7,200 BHP; 15.5 kn; Passengers:
179 in one class; Crew: 137.

1948 Apr 10: Launched.
1949 Jan 10: Delivered.
Jan 18: Maiden voyage Antwerp-
Matadi.
1956 Dec 15: Trials after engine
refit. 9,250 BHP and 16.5
knots after turbocharging.
1967 10,576 GRT.
1968 Mar 20: The *Elisabethville*
was badly damaged by fire at
Antwerp and, as she was not
considered worth repairing, sold to
be broken up.
Dec 27: After the wreck had been
partly broken up at Antwerp, the
hull was towed to the Van Heyghen
Frères breakers' yard at Ghent.

Motorship *Baudouinville*
Compagnie Maritime Belge,
Antwerp

1957 *Thysville*
1961 *Anselm*
1963 *Iberia Star*
1965 *Australasia*

Builders: Cockerill, Hoboken
Yard no: 720
10,946 GRT; 153.7 × 19.6 m /
504 × 64.3 ft; Burmeister & Wain
diesels, Cockerill; Single screw;
7,200 BHP; 15.5 kn; Passengers:
248 in one class; Crew: 140.

1950 Mar 4: Launched.
Sep 7: Delivered.
Sep 19: Maiden voyage Antwerp-
Matadi.
1957 Jun 1: Renamed *Thysville*.
Aug 16: Trials after engine refit.
9,250 BHP and 16.5 knots after
turbocharging.
1961 Sold to Booth Line,
Liverpool. Renamed *Anselm*.
10,868 GRT.
Jun 16: First voyage Liverpool-
South America.
1963 Transferred within the

Vestey Group to Blue Star Line,
London. Renamed *Iberia Star*.
Refitted by Bremer Vulkan.
London-La Plata service.
1965 Renamed *Australasia*.
Placed in Singapore-Melbourne
service for the Austasia Line, a
Vestey company.
1972 Dec 16: From Singapore to
Kaohsiung.
1973 Jul: Broken up at Hualien.

3/4 The Elisabethville *(3) was badly
damaged by fire at Antwerp in March
1968 (4).*
5/6 The Baudouinville *(5) was sold to
England in 1961. Picture 6 shows her
as the* Iberia Star *in 1964.*

3

4

5

6

Motorship *Charlesville*
Compagnie Maritime Belge,
Antwerp

1967 *Georg Büchner*

Builders: Cockerill, Hoboken
Yard no: 743
10,901 GRT; 153.7 × 19.6 m /
504 × 64.3 ft; Burmeister & Wain
diesels, Cockerill; Single screw;
7,200 BHP; 15.5 kn; Passengers:
248 in one class; Crew: 140.

1950 Aug 12: Launched.
1951 Feb 12: Completed.
Feb 15: Delivered.
Mar 6: Maiden voyage Antwerp-
Matadi.
1957 May 18: Engine refit. 9,250
BHP and 16.5 knots after
turbocharging.
1967 Jul 5: Handed over to VEB
Deutsche Seereederei, Rostock,
and renamed *Georg Büchner*.
11,060 GRT.
Commissioned as a cargo vessel in
DSR liner service, the passenger
accommodation being used for
trainee seamen and technicians.

7/8 *The* Charlesville (*7*) *was sold to
Rostock in 1967 and renamed* Georg
Büchner (*8*).

The Pretoria and Edinburgh Castle

Turbine steamer *Pretoria Castle*
Union-Castle Line, London

1966 *S.A. Oranje*

Builders: Harland & Wolff,
Belfast
Yard no: 1332
28,705 GRT; 227.8 × 25.6 m /
747 × 84.0 ft; Geared turbines,
H & W; Twin screw; 35,000 SHP;
22 kn; Passengers: 214 1st class,
541 tourist class; Crew: 400.

1947 Aug 19: Launched.
1948 Jul: Completed.
Southampton-Durban service.
1962 28,625 GRT.
1966 Feb 2: Sold to South African
Marine Corp. Renamed *S.A.
Oranje.* Continued in same service.
1967 27,513 GRT after refit.
1969 Mar 17: The ship was
registered at Cape Town, having
previously had London as her
home port.
1975 Nov 2: Arrived at
Kaohsiung. Broken up there by
Chin Tai Steel Enterprises.

Turbine steamer *Edinburgh Castle*
Union-Castle Line, London

Builders: Harland & Wolff,
Belfast
Yard no: 1333
28,705 GRT; 227.8 × 25.6 m /
747 × 84.0 ft; Geared turbines,
H & W; Twin screw; 35,000 SHP;
22 kn; Passengers: 214 1st class,
541 tourist class; Crew: 400.

1947 Oct 16: Launched.
1948 Nov: Completed.
Dec: Maiden voyage
Southampton-Durban.
1962 28,629 GRT.
1967 27,489 GRT after refit and
modernisation.
1976 Mar 5: Last Durban voyage
with passengers.
Subsequently, one voyage as a
cargo vessel.
May: Sold to Far East interests for
breaking up.
Jun 3: Arrival at Kaohsiung.

1 *Union-Castle Line placed the*
Pretoria Castle *in service in 1948. The
ship was a development of the
company's large pre-war liners.*
2 *The* S.A. Oranje *ex* Pretoria Castle.
3 *The* Edinburgh Castle *after her 1962
refit. Prior to this, the ship had had the
same mast arrangement as the* Pretoria
Castle.

1

2

3

New Ships for Orient Line and P & O

Turbine steamer *Orcades*
Orient Line, London

Builders: Vickers Armstrongs,
Barrow
Yard no: 950
28,164 GRT; 216.0 × 27.6 m /
709 × 90.6 ft; Geared turbines
from builders; Twin screw; 42,500
BHP; 22, max 24.74 kn;
Passengers: 773 1st class, 772
tourist class.

1947 Oct 14: Launched.
1948 Nov 13: Completed.
Dec 14: Maiden voyage London-
Sydney.
1955 Aug 22: First voyage London
via Panama-Australia-via Suez-
London.
1959 Refit of passenger
accommodation. 631 1st class, 734
tourist class. 28,396 GRT.
1960 May 2: P & O Line and
Orient Line pooled their passenger
ships in the same subsidiary
company to form P & O-Orient
Line.
1964 Refitted as a one-class ship
for 1,635 passengers. 28,399 GRT.
1966 Oct: The ship came into the
ownership of P & O Line after the
latter had taken over the balance
of the Orient Line shareholding.
1972 Oct 13: Laid up at
Southampton.
1973 Feb 6: Arrived at Kaohsiung
to be broken up by Nan Feng Steel
Enterprises.

*1/2 Orient Line's first new post-war
liner, the* Orcades.

1

2

Turbine steamer *Himalaya*
P & O Line, London

Builders: Vickers Armstrongs,
Barrow
Yard no: 951
27,955 GRT; 216.0 × 27.6 m /
709 × 90.6 ft; Geared turbines
from builders; Twin screw; 42,500
SHP; 22, max 23.13 kn;
Passengers: 758 1st class, 401
tourist class; Crew: 631.

1948 Oct 5: Launched.
1949 Sep 1: Delivered.
Oct 6: Maiden voyage London-
Sydney.
1956 Aug 30: Five crew members
were killed in an explosion in a
refrigeration chamber.
1958 Service extended beyond
Sydney to San Francisco.
1963 Refitted as a one-class ship
for 1,416 passengers. 27,989 GRT.
1969 28,047 GRT.
1974 Nov 28: Arrived at
Kaohsiung to be broken up.

Turbine steamer *Chusan*
P & O Line, London

Builders: Vickers Armstrongs,
Barrow
Yard no: 964
24,215 GRT; 205.1 × 25.6 m /
673 × 84.0 ft; Geared turbines
from builders; Twin screw; 42,500
SHP; 22 kn; Passengers: 475 1st
class, 551 tourist class; Crew: 572.

1949 Jun 28: Launched.
1950 Jun: Completed.
Jul 1: Maiden voyage, cruising
from Southampton.
Sep 15: First voyage
London-Bombay.
Nov: First voyage London-
Bombay-Japan.
1959/60 Refit of passenger
accommodation. 464 1st class, 541
tourist class. 24,261 GRT.
1960 Service extended beyond
Japan to the USA, and from 1963
occasionally via Australian ports.
1963 24,062 GRT.

1968 24,318 GRT.
1973 Jun 30: Arrived at
Kaohsiung to be broken up.

3/4 The Himalaya *with her original
funnel pattern (3) and with the
Thornycroft funnel cap fitted in 195.
(4).*
5 In 1950 the Chusan *entered the
London-Far East service.*

3

4

5

The Magdalena

Turbine steamer *Magdalena*
Royal Mail Lines, London

Builders: Harland & Wolff,
Belfast
Yard no: 1354
17,547 GRT; 173.8 × 22.3 m /
570 × 73.2 ft; Geared turbines
from builders; Twin screw; 19,800
SHP; 18 kn; Passengers: 133 1st
class, 346 3rd class; Crew: 224.

1948 May 11: Launched.
1949 Feb: Completed.
Mar 9: Maiden voyage London-
Buenos Aires.
Apr 25: On the homeward voyage
Buenos Aires-London the
Magdalena ran onto the Tijucas
rocks off Rio de Janeiro. The
passengers and a part of the crew
were taken off.
Apr 26: The ship was refloated.
During the voyage in tow to Rio de
Janeiro, off Fort São João, the
forepart broke off just forward of
the superstructure and sank. The
rest of the hull was stranded in
Imbui Bay and was sold in June to
a Brazilian firm for breaking up.

1/2 *The* Magdalena *of Royal Mail
Lines was lost after stranding on her
maiden voyage.*

1

2

Blue Funnel Liners

Turbine steamer *Peleus*
Blue Funnel Line, Liverpool

Builders: Cammell Laird,
Birkenhead
Yard no: 1186
10,096 GRT; 157.1 × 20.8 m /
515 × 68.2 ft; Geared turbines
from builders; Single screw;
14,000 SHP; 18.5 kn; Passengers:
31 1st class.

1948 Jul 4: Launched.
1949 Mar: Completed.
Liverpool-Japan service.
1967 The *Peleus* now sailed as a
cargo liner. 10,068 GRT.
1968 Measurement 9,747 GRT.
1972 Jul 13: Arrived at Kaohsiung
to be broken up by Li Chon Steel
Enterprise Co Ltd.

Turbine steamer *Patroclus*
Blue Funnel Line, Liverpool

1972 Philoctetes

Builders: Vickers-Armstrong,
Newcastle
Yard no: 110
10,109 GRT; 157.2 × 20.8 m /
516 × 68.2 ft; Geared turbines
from builders; Single screw;
15,000 SHP; 18.5 kn; Passengers:
31 1st class.

1949 Jul 8: Launched.
1950 Jan 18: Completed.
Liverpool-Japan service.
1967 Used only as a cargo liner.
9,754 GRT.
1972 Nov: Renamed *Philoctetes*.
1973 Feb 12: Arrived at
Kaohsiung. Broken up by Chin Tai
Enterprise Co.

Turbine steamer *Perseus*
Blue Funnel Line, Liverpool

Builders: Vickers-Armstrong,
Newcastle
Yard no: 111
10,109 GRT; 157.2 × 20.8 m /
516 × 68.2 ft; Geared turbines
from builders; Single screw;
15,000 SHP; 18.5 kn; Passengers:
31 1st class.

1949 Oct 22: Launched.
1950 Apr 4: Completed.
Liverpool-Japan service.
1967 Used only as a cargo liner.
9,753 GRT.
1973 Jan 3: Arrived at Kaohsiung
to be broken up.

Turbine steamer *Pyrrhus*
Blue Funnel Line, Liverpool

Builders: Cammell Laird,
Birkenhead
10,093 GRT; 157.1 × 20.8 m /
515 × 68.2 ft; Geared turbines
from builders; Single screw;
15,000 SHP; 18.5 kn; Passengers:
31 1st class.

1948 Oct 12: Launched.
1949 Aug: Completed.
Liverpool-Japan service.
1959 Oct 7: Rescued crew of
sinking Panama-registered
Malaya north of Hong Kong.
1964 Nov 16/17: On fire at
Liverpool.
Repaired at North Shields when
passenger accommodation was
removed. 10,060 GRT.
1968 9,626 GRT.
1972 Sep 16: Arrived at
Kaohsiung to be broken up.

1-4 *The Blue Funnel Line had the
sister ships* Pyrrhus (*1*), Peleus (*2*),
Patroclus (*3*) *and* Perseus (*4*) *built for
the Liverpool-Japan service.*

2

3

4

Turbine steamer *Helenus*
Blue Funnel Line, Liverpool

Builders: Harland & Wolff,
Belfast
Yard no: 1376
10,125 GRT; 159.2 × 21.1 m /
522 × 69.2 ft; Geared turbines,
H & W; Single screw; 15,000 SHP;
18.25 kn; Passengers: 30 1st class.

1949 Apr 13: Launched.
Oct: Completed.
Nov 14: Maiden voyage Liverpool-
Brisbane.
1964 Used only as a cargo liner.
1969 9,717 GRT.
1972 Jul 7: Arrived at Kaohsiung
to be broken up.

Turbine steamer *Jason*
Blue Funnel Line, Liverpool

Builders: Swan, Hunter &
Wigham Richardson, Newcastle
Yard no: 1775
10,160 GRT; 159.2 × 21.1 m /
522 × 69.2 ft; Geared turbines
from builders; Single screw;
15,000 SHP; 18.25 kn; Passengers:
30 1st class.

1949 Jun 9: Launched.
1950 Jan: Completed.
Feb 18: Maiden voyage Liverpool-
Brisbane.
1964 Used only as a cargo liner.
1968 9,715 GRT.
1972 May: To Kaohsiung to be
broken up.

5/6 *A second Blue Funnel Line
foursome for the Australia service
consisted of the* Helenus *(5),* Jason *(6),*
Hector *and* Ixion.

6

Turbine steamer *Hector*
Blue Funnel Line, Liverpool

Builders: Harland & Wolff,
Belfast
Yard no: 1377
10,125 GRT; 159.2 × 21.1 m /
522 × 69.2 ft; Geared turbines,
H & W; Single screw; 15,000 SHP;
18.25 kn; Passengers: 30 1st class.

1949 Jul 27: Launched.
1950 Mar: Completed.
Apr 5: Maiden voyage Liverpool-
Brisbane.
1964 Used only as a cargo liner.
1968 9,718 GRT.
1972 Jul 2: Arrived at Kaohsiung
to be broken up.

Turbine steamer *Ixion*
Blue Funnel Line, Liverpool

Builders: Harland & Wolff,
Belfast
Yard no: 1417
10,125 GRT; 159.2 × 21.1 m /
522 × 69.2 ft; Geared turbines;
H & W; Single screw; 15,000 SHP;
18.25 kn; Passengers: 30 1st class.

1950 Jul 28: Launched.
1951 Jan: Completed.
Jan 24: Maiden voyage Liverpool-
Brisbane.
1964 Used only as a cargo liner.
1968 9,724 GRT.
1972 Feb 13: Arrived at
Barcelona. Broken up by
Salvamento y Demolicion SA.

7/8 *The Blue Funnel liners* Hector (*7*)
and Ixion (*8*).

Motorship *Lavoisier*
Chargeurs Réunis, Le Havre

1961 *Riviera Prima*
1964 *Viking Princess*

Builders: A et Ch de la Loire, St Nazaire
11,968 GRT; 163.6 × 19.6 m / 537 × 64.3 ft; Sulzer diesels, Constr Mec; Twin screw; 12,000 BHP; 17, max 18.7 kn; Passengers: 94 1st class, 230 2nd class.

1948 Oct 30: Launched.
1950 Completed.
Sep 19: Maiden voyage Le Havre-Buenos Aires. Then placed in Hamburg-Buenos Aires service.
1961 Aug: Sold to Commerciale Marittime Petroli SpA, Palermo. Rebuilt at Genoa for cruising. Renamed *Riviera Prima*.
1962 Nov:Entered service as cruise liner. 12,812 GRT.
1964 Oct: Sold to A/S Sigline, Berge Sigval Bergesen, Oslo.

Renamed *Viking Princess*.
1965 Cruising in the Caribbean.
1966 Apr 8: During a cruise in the Caribbean a fire broke out in the engine room and became out of control. The crew and passengers abandoned ship and were picked up by the German *Cap Norte,* the Liberian *Navigator* and the Chinese *Chunking Victory.* Two passengers died of heart attacks. The *Navigator* towed the *Viking Princess* to Port Royal, Jamaica. The wreck was sold to be broken up at Bilbao.

Motorship *Claude Bernard*
Chargeurs Réunis, Le Havre

1962 *J.G. Fichte*

Builders: A et Ch de la Loire, St Nazaire
12,021 GRT; 163.4 × 19.6 m / 535 × 64.3 ft; Sulzer diesels, Constr Mec; 12,000 BHP; Twin screw; 17, max 19 kn; Passengers: 94 1st class, 230 2nd class.

1948 Oct 1: The launching planned for this date had to be postponed because of a strike. Oct 31: Launched.
1950 Completed.
Mar 18: Maiden voyage Le Havre-Buenos Aires. Then Hamburg-Buenos Aires service.
1962 Aug 7: Taken over by VEB Deutsche Seereederei, Rostock. Renamed *J.G. Fichte.* The liner was no longer used as a passenger ship, but served as a training vessel. 11,942 GRT.
1972 11,045 GRT.

1

2

3

1/2 *Built for the South America service of Chargeurs Réunis, the* Lavoisier (1) *was sold to Norway in 1964 and renamed* Viking Princess (2).
3 *The* Claude Bernard, *built in 1950.*

Motorship *Laënnec*
Cie Sudatlantique, Bordeaux

1966 *Belle Abeto*

Builders: A et Ch de la Loire, St
Nazaire
12,007 GRT; 163.9 × 19.6 m /
538 × 64.3 ft; Sulzer diesels,
Constr Mec; Twin screw; 12,000
BHP; 17, max 19 kn; Passengers:
110 1st class, 326 3rd class.

1951 Feb 25: Launched.
1952 Jan 16: Maiden voyage Le
Havre-Buenos Aires, then
Hamburg-La Plata service.
1962 Sep 20: Handed over to
Messageries Maritimes. Same
service.
1966 Sold to Cia de Nav Abeto
SA, Panama. Renamed *Belle
Abeto*.
Entered Indonesia-Jeddah route
after refit for pilgrim service.
12,177 GRT.

1976 Jul 30: Badly damaged by
fire in Sasebo; sank in the harbour
the following day.

Motorship *Charles Tellier*
Cie Sudatlantique, Bordeaux

1967 *Le Havre Abeto*

Builders: A et Ch de La Loire, St
Nazaire
12,007 GRT; 163.9 × 19.6 m /
538 × 64.3 ft; Sulzer diesels,
Constr Mec; Twin screw; 12,000
BHP; 17, max 19 kn; Passengers:
110 1st class, 326 3rd class.

1951 Dec 2: Launched.
1952 Jul 28: Delivered.
Aug 2: Maiden voyage Bordeaux-
Buenos Aires, then Hamburg-La
Plata service.

1962 Nov 3: Handed over to
Messageries Maritimes. Same
service.
1967 Sold to Cia de Nav Abeto
SA, Panama. Renamed *Le Havre
Abeto*. Entered Indonesia-Red Sea
pilgrim service after refit. 12,177
GRT.

*4/6 Cie Sudatlantique had two further
ships of this class built, the* Laënnec
(4) and the Charles Tellier *(5). The
latter is shown in the Messageries
Maritimes colours in 1963 (6).*

4

Turbine steamer *Presidente Peron*
Cia Argentina de Nav Dodero,
Buenos Aires

1955 *Argentina*

Builders: Vickers-Armstrong,
Barrow
Yard no: 969
12,459 GRT; 161.5 × 21.7 m /
530 × 71.2 ft; Geared turbines
from builders; Twin screw; 14,500
SHP; 18, max 19.5 kn; Passengers:
74 1st class; Crew: 145.

1948 Nov 3: Launched.
1949 Jun: Completed.
Jul: Maiden voyage
London-Buenos Aires; later from
Hamburg.
1955 After the fall of the Peron
government the ship was renamed
Argentina and managed by the
Flota Argentina de Navegacion de
Ultramar.
1962 The FANU and the Flota
Mercante del Estado amalgamated
to form the Empresa Lineas
Maritimas Argentinas.
1966 Used only as a cargo vessel.
1969 Jul 31: Laid up at Rosario.
1971 Put up for sale.

1973 Jan 19: The *Argentina* left
Rosario for Campana, where she
was broken up.

Turbine steamer *Eva Peron*
Cia Argentina de Nav Dodero,
Buenos Aires

1955 *Uruguay*

Builders: Vickers-Armstrong,
Barrow
Yard no: 970
12,627 GRT; 161.5 × 21.7 m /
530 × 71.2 ft; Geared turbines
from builders; Twin screw; 14,500
SHP; 18, max 19.7 kn; Passengers:
96 1st class; Crew: 145.

1949 Aug 25: Launched.
1950 Apr: Completed.
May 9: Maiden voyage
London-Buenos Aires; later from
Hamburg.
1955 Renamed *Uruguay* after fall
of Peron government, and
managed by the FANU.
1962 FANU and Flota Mercante

del Estado amalgamated to form
ELMA.
1967 Used only as a cargo vessel.
1969 Oct 21: Laid up at Rosario.
1973 Jan 16: Arrived at San Pedro
to be broken up.

1 *The* Argentina *ex* Presidente Peron
with the funnel markings of the
ELMA.
2/4 The Eva Peron, *photograph 1950*
(2), was renamed Uruguay *in 1955 (3),*
photograph 1960. Picture 4 shows the
ship in 1961 with black hull and FANU
funnel.

1

2

3

4

Turbine steamer *17 de Octubre*
Cia Argentina de Nav Dodero,
Buenos Aires

1955 *Libertad*

Builders: Vickers-Armstrong,
Barrow
Yard no: 971
12,634 GRT; 161.5 × 21.7 m /
530 × 71.2 ft; Geared turbines
from builders; Twin screw; 14,500
SHP; 18, max 19 kn; Passengers:
96 1st class; Crew: 145.

1950 Apr 4: Launched.
Oct: Completed.
London-Buenos Aires service; later
from Hamburg.
1955 Renamed *Libertad* after the
fall of the Peron government.
Managed by FANU.
1962 FANU and Flota Mercante
del Estado amalgamated to form
ELMA.
1963/64 Refitted as a one-class
ship, 400 tourist class. 12,653
GRT.
1974 Jan 15: Laid up at Villa
Constitucion.
1975 Sold to be broken up in
Argentina. Scrapped at Campana.

Motorship *Rio de la Plata*
Flota Mercante del Estado,
Buenos Aires

Builders: Ansaldo, Sestri-Ponente
Yard no: 890
11,317 GRT; 167.5 × 20.0 m /
550 × 65.6 ft; FIAT diesels; Twin
screw; 18,400 BHP; 18.5, max
20 kn; Passengers: 116 1st class;
Crew: 155.

1949 Mar 6: Launched.
1950 Apr: Completed.
Buenos Aires-New York service.
1962 Flota Mercante del Estado
and FANU amalgamated to form
ELMA.
1963 Refitted for Buenos Aires-
Hamburg service. 372 tourist class
passengers.
1964 Nov 19: While lying at the
Demarchi yards at Buenos Aires
for repairs the *Rio de la Plata* was
completely burnt out.
1968 Broken up at Buenos Aires.

Motorship *Rio Jachal*
Flota Mercante del Estado,
Buenos Aires

Builders: Ansaldo, Sestri-Ponente
Yard no: 891
11,342 GRT; 167.5 × 20.0 m /
550 × 65.6 ft; FIAT diesels,
Ansaldo; Twin screw; 18,400 BHP;
18.5, max 20 kn; Passengers: 116
1st class; Crew: 155.

1949 May 12: Launched.
1950 Sep: Completed. Buenos
Aires-New York service.
1962 Flota Mercante del Estado
and FANU amalgamated to form
ELMA.
1962 Sep 28: Badly damaged by
fire at New York.
1964 Apr 25: To Buenos Aires
after temporary repairs and laid up
there.
1968 Apr 17: Caught fire again.
1969 Sold to be broken up.
1970 Broken up at Buenos Aires.

5

5 *The* Libertad *after her 1964 refit.*
6/7 *The motorship* Rio de la Plata (6)
and Rio Jachal (7) *of the Argentinian*
Flota Mercante del Estado.

Motorship *Rio Tunuyan*
Flota Mercante del Estado,
Buenos Aires

1952 *Evita*
1955 *Rio Tunuyan*

Builders: Ansaldo, Sestri-Ponente
Yard no: 895
11,317 GRT; 167.5 × 20.0 m /
550 × 65.6 ft; FIAT diesels,
Ansaldo; Twin screw; 18,400 BHP;
18.5, max 20 kn; Passengers: 116
1st class; Crew: 155.

1949 Oct 30: Launched.
1951 Apr: Completed.
Buenos Aires-New York service.
1952 Renamed *Evita*.
1955 Renamed *Rio Tunuyan*.
1962 Flota Mercante and FANU
amalgamated to form ELMA.
1963/64 Refitted as a one-class
ship. 372 tourist class. 11,433
GRT.
1964 First voyage Buenos Aires-
Hamburg.
1972 Jan 30: Laid up at Villa
Constitucion.

8/9 *The* Rio Tunuyan *on the Elbe in
1970.*

Rangitoto and Rangitane

Motorship *Rangitoto*
New Zealand Line, London

1969 Oriental Carnaval

Builders: Vickers-Armstrong,
Newcastle
Yard no: 109
21,809 GRT; 185.6 × 23.8 m /
609 × 78.1 ft; Doxford diesels from
builders; Twin screw; 16,000
SHP; 17 kn; Passengers: 416 in
one class.

1949 Jan 12: Launched.
Aug: Completed.
Aug 25: Maiden voyage
London-Wellington.
1967 To Federal SN Co.
Continued in same service.
1969 Aug: Sold to Oriental South
American Lines Inc, Monrovia,
which was a part of the Tung
group. Renamed *Oriental*
Carnaval.
1970 Apr: First voyage in
round-the-world service from San
Diego. 16,661 GRT.

1/3 *The* Rangitoto *in her original form*
as a New Zealand liner (1), as a
Federal liner in 1967 (2) without the
mainmast (removed in 1965) and as the
Oriental Carnaval *in 1970 (3).*

1

2

3

Motorship *Rangitane*
New Zealand Line, London

1968 *Jan*
1968 *Oriental Esmeralda*

Builders: Brown, Clydebank
Yard no: 648
21,867 GRT; 185.6 × 23.8 m /
609 × 78.1 ft; Doxford diesels,
Brown; Twin screw; 15,500 BHP;
17 kn; Passengers: 416 in one
class.

1949 Jun 30: Launched.
Dec: Completed.
1950 Jan 27: Maiden voyage
London-Wellington.
1967 To Federal SN Co.
Continued in same service.
1968 May: Sold to Astroguardo
Cia Nav, Piraeus. Renamed *Jan*.
The ship made one voyage only to
Formosa under this name.
Sep: Arrived at Kaohsiung to be
broken up, then sold to the Tung
group. Renamed *Oriental
Esmeralda*. Registered for
Oriental Latin American Lines
Inc, Monrovia.
1969 Jan: Refitted at Hong Kong
for round-the-world service.
Jun 4: First voyage from San
Diego. 19,567 GRT.

4/5 *The* Rangitane *(4) became the*
Oriental Esmeralda *(5) in 1968.*

4

5

The Oslofjord

Motorship *Oslofjord*
Norwegian America Line, Oslo

1969 *Fulvia*

Builders: Nederlandsche Sb Mij,
Amsterdam
Yard no: 410
16,844 GRT; 175.9 × 22.0 m /
577 × 72.2 ft; Stork diesels; Twin
screw; 16,350 BHP; 20, max
21.74 kn; Passengers: 266 1st
class, 359 tourist class.

1949 Apr 2: Launched.
Nov: Completed.
Nov 26: Maiden voyage Oslo-New
York. Also cruising.
1966/67 Modernised and refitted
by the builders during the winter
months. 16,923 GRT.
1969 The *Oslofjord* was chartered
for three years to the Italian
shipping company Costa
Armatori, which renamed the ship
Fulvia and used her for cruising.
1970 Jul 20: While carrying a full
complement of 721 the *Fulvia*
caught fire 100 nautical miles
north of the Canary Islands after
an explosion in the engine room.
The French liner *Ancerville,* which
had been summoned to assist,
picked up the crew and passengers
of the helpless ship.
Jul 20: The *Fulvia* sank in position
29° 57'N-16° 30 W during an
attempt to tow her to Teneriffe.

*1/2 The first new post-war passenger
ship of the Norwegian America Line
was the* Oslofjord *(1), completed in
1949 but burnt out in 1970 while
serving under charter to an Italian
company as the* Fulvia *(2).*

Diesel-electric vessel *Skaugum*
I.M. Skaugen, Oslo

Launched as *Ostmark*
1964 *Ocean Builder*

Builders: Germaniawerft, Kiel
Yard no: 747; Howaldt Kiel
11,626 GRT; 168.1 × 20.3 m /
552 × 66.6 ft; Diesel-electric
machinery from Germaniawerft;
Twin screw; 16,000 BHP; 15, max
18 kn; Passengers: 1,700 in one
class.

1940 Jan 17: Launched as the fast
cargo liner *Ostmark* for the
Hamburg-America Line. Laid up
incomplete during the war.
1945 May: British war prize.
1948 Sold by the British Ministry
of Transport to I.M. Skaugen, who
had the ship rebuilt as an emigrant
carrier at the Howaldt yard, Kiel.
The vessel had lain incomplete at
the yard for eight years. Renamed
Skaugum.
1949 Apr: Completed. The
Skaugum was placed in the
emigrant service between Genoa
and Australia.
1957 Rebuilt as a cargo vessel at
the Howaldt yard. New engines,
direct diesels, 8,100 BHP, 15
knots. 11,111 GRT.
1964 Sold to Ocean Shipping &
Enterprises, Monrovia. Renamed
Ocean Builder.
1965 10,998 GRT.
1972 Aug 25: Arrived at
Kaohsiung. Broken up by Chien
Tai Iron Works.

Motorship *Surriento*
Achille Lauro, Naples

Ex *Barnett*
Ex *Santa Maria*

Builders:Furness SB Co, Haverton
Yard no: 104
10,699 GRT; 151.8 × 19.5 m /
498 × 64.0 ft; Sulzer diesels; Twin
screw; 8,000 BHP; 17 kn;
Passengers: 187 1st class, 868
tourist class.

1927 Aug 15: Launched as *Santa
Maria* for Grace Line, New York.
1928 Apr: Completed. Grace Line
placed the ship in the New York-
Central America service. 8,153
GRT. 150 1st class passengers.
1940 Aug: Sold to the US Navy.
Sep 25: Renamed *Barnett*. Type
Designation number: AP 11.
1943 Feb 1: Number: APA 5.
Jul 11: Seven killed by bomb hit off
Sicily.
1946 Jul: Laid up.
1948 Bought by Achille Lauro.
Renamed *Surriento*. Large scale
refit at Genoa.
1949 May: First voyage Genoa-
Sydney.
1951 First voyage
Naples-Venezuela.
1953 Australia service again.
1957 Naples-Venezuela service
again.
1959/60 Refitted and modernised
at Genoa. 1,080 tourist class
passengers.
1965 10,928 GRT.
1966 Sep 30: Arrived at La Spezia
to be broken up.

1/2 The Skaugum *(1) was launched in
1940 as the Hamburg-America Line
cargo liner* Ostmark *(2).*

3

4

3/4 *The* Surriento (3) *originated from the already 20 years old American* Santa Maria. *She was rebuilt again in 1959 (4).*

Turbine steamer *Corrientes*
Cia Argentina de Nav Dodero,
Buenos Aires

Ex *Tracker*

Builders: Seattle Tacoma SB Corp,
Tacoma
Yard no: 17
12,053 GRT; 150.0 × 21.1 m /
492 × 69.2 ft; Allis-Chalmers
geared turbines; Single screw;
9,350 SHP; 16.5, max 17 kn;
Passengers: 4 1st class, 1,338
tourist class; Crew: 192.

1941 Laid down as cargo liner
Mormacmail for Moore-
McCormack Lines.
1942 Mar 7: Launched as
auxiliary aircraft carrier for the US
Navy.
May: Building continued for the
Royal Navy.
1943 Commissioned as HMS
Tracker.
1945 Handed back to the USA.
1948 Sold to the Newport News
shipyard.
1949 Bought by Dodero.
Renamed *Corrientes*. Refitted as a
passenger ship at Newport News.
Buenos Aires-Genoa service.
1955 Management transferred to
FANU.
1962 Amalgamation of FANU and
Flota Mercante del Estado to form
ELMA.
1964 Aug 1:The *Corrientes* had to
put in to Lisbon because of engine
damage. This proved so extensive
that the ship was sold in
September to Belgian breakers.
Sep 14: Arrived at Antwerp.

Turbine steamer *Salta*
Cia Argentina de Nav Dodero,
Buenos Aires

Ex *Shah*
Ex *Jamaica*

Builders: Seattle Tacoma SB Corp,
Seattle
Yard no: 38
12,053 GRT; 150.0 × 21.1 m /
492 × 69.2 ft; Allis-Chalmers
geared turbines; Single screw;
9,350 SHP; 16.5, max 17 kn;
Passengers: 4 1st class, 1,338
tourist class; Crew: 192.

1942 Jul 20: Launched as the
auxiliary aircraft carrier *Jamaica*
for the US Navy.
1943 Apr 21: Commissioned.
Sep 27: Handed over to the Royal
Navy. Renamed *Shah.*
1945 Dec 6: Returned to the USA.
1948 Sold to the Newport News
shipyard.
1949 Bought by Dodero.
Renamed *Salta* and rebuilt as a
passenger ship at Newport News.
Buenos Aires-Genoa service.
1955 Managed by FANU.
1962 FANU and Flota Mercante
del Estado amalgamated to form
ELMA.
1964 Dec: Laid up at Buenos
Aires because of boiler damage.
1966 Jun: Sold to be broken up at
Buenos Aires.

5

6

7

5/7 *The turbine steamers* Corrientes
(5) and Salta *(6) served as auxiliary
aircraft carriers during the Second
World War. Picture 7 shows HMS*
Tracker, *later the* Corrientes.

Motorship *Anna Salén*
Sven Salén, Stockholm

Ex *Empire Lagan*
Ex *Archer*
Ex *Mormacland*
1955 *Tasmania*
1961 *Union Reliance*

Builders: Sun SB & DD Co,
Chester
Yard no: 184
11,672 GRT; 150.5 × 21.1 m /
494 × 69.2 ft; Busch-Sulzer
geared diesels; Single screw; 9,000
BHP; 17 kn; Passengers: 600 in
one class.

1939 Dec 14: Launched as C3
cargo liner *Mormacland* for
Moore-McCormack Lines.
1940 Taken over before
completion by the US Navy.

Refitted as an auxiliary aircraft
carrier.
1941 Sep: Commissioned by the
Royal Navy as HMS *Archer*.
1942 Jan 13: The *Archer* collided
with the American steamship
Brazos, which sank. The badly
damaged aircraft carrier was
towed back to Charleston stern
first.
1945 The *Archer* was taken over
by the Ministry of War Transport
and refitted as a cargo vessel.
Managed by the Blue Funnel Line.
1946 Renamed *Empire Lagan*.
13,399 GRT. Returned to the US
Maritime Commission. Bought by
Sven Salén. The ship was
registered under the ownership of
the Rederi A/S Pulp and rebuilt as
a passenger ship, the *Anna Salén*.

1949 In service as an emigrant
ship. Used on various routes.
1955 Sold to Cia Nav Tasmania,
Piraeus. Renamed *Tasmania* and
placed in the Piraeus-Melbourne
service of Hellenic Mediterranean
Lines.
1958 7,638 GRT.
1961 Sold to China Union Lines,
Taipeh. Renamed *Union Reliance*.
Nov 7: The *Union Reliance*
collided with the Norwegian tanker
Beran in the Houston Ship
Channel and was beached on fire.
Nov 11: The ship was towed to
Galveston.
1962 Jan: Sold to be broken up at
New Orleans.

8 *The* Anna Salén, *too, served as an
auxiliary aircraft carrier during the
Second World War.*

Motorship *Fairsea*
Alvion SS Corp, Panama

Ex *Charger*
Ex *Rio de la Plata*

Builders: Sun SB & DD Co,
Chester
Yard no: 188
11,678 GRT; 150.0 m × 21.1 m /
492 × 69.2 ft; Doxford geared
diesels, Sun; Single screw; 9,000
BHP; 16, max 17 kn; Passengers:
1,800 in one class.

1941 Mar 1: Launched as C3
cargo and passenger vessel for
Moore-McCormack Lines.
Oct 4: Building continued for the
US Navy as the auxiliary aircraft
carrier *Charger*.
1942 Mar 3: Completed. Handed
over to the Royal Navy.
1946 Mar 15: Released from naval
service.
1949 Bought by Alvion SS Corp.
Renamed *Fairsea*. Rebuilt as a
passenger ship.
1950 First voyage Bremerhaven-
Sydney.
1953 Apr 30: Bremerhaven-
Quebec service, then again
Bremerhaven-Sydney.
1955 Dec 6: First voyage
Southampton-Sydney.
1957/58 Refitted and modernised
at Trieste. 13,432 GRT. 1,460
tourist class passengers.
Registered under the name of
Sitmar Line, Genoa.
1958 Apr: Southampton-Sydney
service again.
1968 Registered in Panama for
Passenger Liner Services Inc.
13,317 GRT.
1969 Jan 29: During a voyage
from Sydney to Southampton the
Fairsea was west of Balboa when
she was disabled through a fire in
the engine room. The American
vessel *Louise Lykes* towed the
Fairsea to Balboa where she was
laid up.
Aug 6: Arrived at La Spezia under
the tow of the Italian tug *Vortice* to
be broken up.

9/10 *The* Fairsea *about 1950 (9) and
after her 1958 rebuilding (10).*

Turbine steamer *Roma*
Achille Lauro, Naples

Ex *Atheling*
Ex *Glacier*

Builders: Seattle-Tacoma SB
Corp, Tacoma
Yard no: 28
14,687 GRT; 150.0 × 21.1 m /
492 × 69.2 ft; Allis-Chalmers
geared turbines; Single screw;
9,350 SHP; 17 kn; Passengers: 92
1st class, 680 tourist class.

1942 Sep 7: Launched as auxiliary
aircraft carrier *Glacier* for the US
Navy. Had been laid down as a C3
cargo vessel.
1943 Jul 31: Handed over to the
Royal Navy after completion.
Renamed *Atheling*.
1946 Dec: Returned to the US
Navy.
1947 Nov: Sold to a US company.
1950 Bought by Lauro. Rebuilt at
Genoa as a passenger ship.
1951 Aug: First voyage Genoa-
Sydney.
1953 May: First voyage
Naples-New York.
1956 Dec: Genoa-Sydney service
again.
1960 After passenger
accommodation refit: 119 1st
class, 1,026 tourist class. 14,976
GRT.
1966 First voyage Naples-La
Guaira.
1967 Broken up at Savona.

Turbine steamer *Sydney*
Achille Lauro, Naples

Ex *Fencer*
1967 *Roma*
1971 *Galaxy Queen*
1972 *Lady Dina*
1973 *Caribia 2*

Builders: Western Pipe & Steel Co,
San Francisco
Yard no: 77
14,708 GRT; 150.0 × 21.1 m /
492 × 69.2 ft; General Electric
geared turbines; Single screw;
9,350 SHP; 17 kn; Passengers: 94
1st class, 708 tourist class.

1942 Laid down as the auxiliary
aircraft carrier *Croatan* for the US
Navy. Originally intended as a C3
cargo vessel.
Apr 9: Launched as HMS *Fencer*.
1943 Feb 27: Commissioned by
the Royal Navy.
1946 Dec 21: Returned to the US
Navy.
1950 Bought by Achille Lauro.
Renamed *Sydney*. Rebuilt at
Genoa as a passenger ship.
1951 Sep: First voyage Genoa-
Sydney.
1953 Four voyages Liverpool-
Canada, then Australia service
again.
1960 Passengers: 119 1st class,
994 tourist class. 14,986 GRT.
1966 First voyage Naples-La
Guaira.
1967 Renamed *Roma*. Cruising
exclusively.
1969 Sold to Aretusa SpA di Nav,
Rome. Cruising.
1970 Oct: Laid up at La Spezia.
Sold to Sovereign Cruise Ships Ltd,
Famagusta.
1971 Renamed *Galaxy Queen*.
Mediterranean cruises.

1972 To G. Kotzovilis. Renamed
Lady Dina.
1973 To Marimina Shipping Co
SA as *Cariba 2*.
1974 Sold to Terrestre Marittima,
La Spezia, to be broken up.
1975 Sep 1: Scrapping
commenced.

11

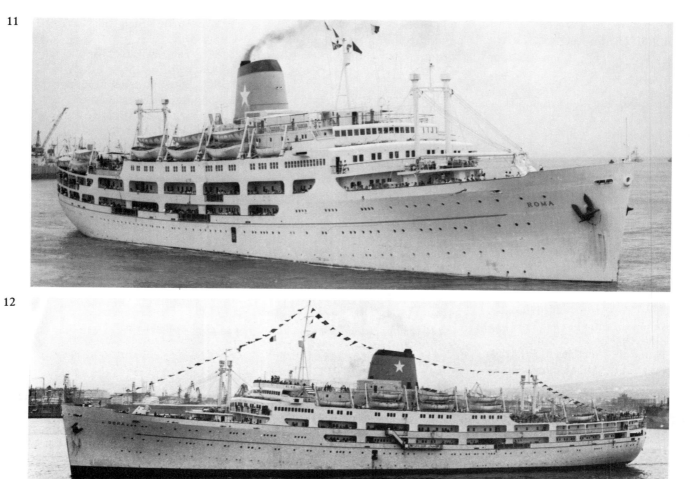

12

13

Motorship *Nelly*
Caribbean Land & Shipping Corp,
Panama

Ex *Long Island*
Ex *Mormacmail*
1955 *Seven Seas*

Builders: Sun SB & DD Co,
Chester
Yard no: 184
11,086 GRT; 150.0 × 21.2 m /
492 × 69.6 ft; Busch-Sulzer
geared diesels; Single screw; 9,000
BHP; 16.5, max 17 kn;
Passengers: 1,300 in one class;
Crew: 192.

1940 Jan 11: Launched as C3
cargo liner *Mormacmail* for
Moore-McCormack Lines, New
York.
1941 Mar 6: To the US Navy
shortly before completion. Refitted
as an auxiliary aircraft carrier at

Newport News.
1941 Jun 2: Commissioned by the
US Navy as the *Long Island*.
1946 Mar 26: Released from
service.
1947 Apr: Sold to be broken up,
but laid up.
1948 Mar 12: Bought by
Caribbean Land & Shipping and
rebuilt as a passenger ship.
1949 Renamed *Nelly*. Entered
Bremerhaven-Melbourne service.
1953 Refitted for North Atlantic
service and renamed *Seven Seas*.
1955 Apr 30: First voyage
Bremerhaven-Montreal. 12,575
GRT. 20 1st class, 987 tourist
class.
Sold to Europa-Canada-Line,
Bremen, in the autumn of the
same year. Apart from the Canada
service the *Seven Seas* also
undertook study cruises for the

Seven Seas University, Whittier,
California.
1963 Apr: Bremerhaven-New
York service.
1965 Jul 18: After a fire in the
engine room the *Seven Seas* drifted
out of control in the Atlantic. The
Dutch tug *Ierse Zee* and the US
Coast Guard vessel *Absecon* towed
the liner to St John. Not ready for
service again until June 1966.
1966 Sep: The *Seven Seas* was sold
to become a students'
accommodation ship at
Rotterdam.
Sep 24: Arrived at Parkhaven.

11/12 *The two Lauro liners* Roma (*11*)
and Sydney. *When the former was
sold, the latter, her sister ship, was
given the name* Roma (*12*).
13/14 *The* Nelly *about 1950 (13) and in
1960 as the* Seven Seas (*14*).

14

The Bloemfontein Castle

Motorship *Bloemfontein Castle*
Union-Castle Line, London

1959 *Patris*

Builders: Harland & Wolff,
Belfast
Yard no: 1421
18,400 GRT; 181.3 × 23.3 m /
595 × 76.4 ft; Burmeister & Wain
diesels, H & W; Twin screw;
20,000 BHP; 18.5 kn; Passengers:
721 cabin class.

1949 Aug 25: Launched.
1950 Mar: Completed.
Apr 6: Maiden voyage London-
Beira.
1953 Jan 8: The *Bloemfontein
Castle* took on board the crew and
passengers of the Dutch liner
Klipfontein, which was sinking off
Mozambique.
1959 Nov: Sold to Chandris Bros.
Renamed *Patris*. Registered at
Piraeus in the name of the
National Greek Australian Line.
Passenger accommodation refitted
at North Shields. 36 1st class,
1,000 tourist class. 16,259 GRT.
Dec 14: First voyage Piraeus-
Sydney.
1972 Cruising from Australian
ports and Australia-Singapore
service.
1975 Feb 14: Arrived at the city of
Darwin, which had been destroyed
by a tropical storm. Served as
accommdation ship until
November.

1 *The Union-Castle motorship*
Bloemfontein Castle.

1

Turbine steamer *Diemerdyk*
Holland-America Line, Rotterdam

1968 *Oriental Amiga*

Builders: Wilton-Fijenoord,
Schiedam
Yard no: 723
11,195 GRT; 151.9 × 21.1 m /
498 × 69.2 ft; Geared turbines,
General Electric; Single screw;
8,500 SHP; 16.5 kn; Passengers:
61 in one class.

1949 Dec 17: Launched.
1950 Completed.
Jun: Maiden voyage
Rotterdam-New York. Then
Hamburg-North American West
Coast.
1968 Sold to the Tung group.
Registered in the name of Oriental
Africa Line, Monrovia.
Renamed *Oriental Amiga.*
Dec: First voyage in Los Angeles-
Hong Kong service.

1970 10,150 GRT.
1974 Registered in the name of
Chinese Maritime Trust, Taipeh.

1/2 The Diemerdyk *as a
Holland-America liner (1) and in 1970
as the* Oriental Amiga *(2).*

Turbine steamer *President Jackson*
American President Lines,
San Francisco

1951 *Barrett*
1973 *Empire State V*

Builders: New York SB Co,
Camden
Yard no: 485
12,660 GRT; 162.5 × 22.3 m /
533 × 73.2 ft; Geared turbines,
General Electric; Single screw;
13,750 SHP; 19, max 21.5 kn;
Passengers: 392 cabin class, 1,500
troops.

1950 Jun 27: Launched.
1951 Intended for American
President Lines' passenger service,
the ship was taken over by the US
Navy. Continued as a troop
transport. Renamed *Barrett*.
Type Designation number: T-AP
196.
Dec 15: Delivered.
1973 Jul 1: Removed from list of
US Navy ships.
Sep 5: New York State Maritime
College as a training vessel.
Renamed *Empire State V.*

Turbine steamer *President Adams*
American President Lines,
San Francisco

1951 *Geiger*

Builders: New York SB Co,
Camden
Yard no: 486
12,660 GRT; 162.5 × 22.3 m /
533 × 73.2 ft; Geared turbines,
General Electric; Single screw;
13,750 SHP; 19, max 21 kn;
Passengers: 392 cabins, 1,500
troops.

1950 Oct 9: Launched.
1951 The US Navy took over the
incomplete ship and building
continued as a troop transport.
Renamed *Geiger*. Number: T-AP
197.
1952 Sep 13: Delivered.
1957 Sep: The *Geiger* rescued
survivors from the German sail
training ship *Pamir* which had
sunk in a hurricane.
1971 Apr 26: Laid up at Suisun.

Turbine steamer *President Hayes*
American President Lines,
San Francisco

1951 *Upshur*

Builders: New York SB Co,
Camden
Yard no: 487
12,660 GRT; 162.5 × 22.3 m /
533 × 73.2 ft; Geared turbines,
General Electric; Single screw;
13,750 SHP; 19, max 21 kn;
Passengers: 392 cabins, 1,500
troops.

1951 Jan 19: Launched.
The incomplete ship was taken
over by the US Navy and building
continued as a troop transport.
Renamed *Upshur*. Number: T-AP
198.
1952 Dec 20: Delivered.
1973 Sold to the US Dept of
Commerce.
The ship was placed at the disposal
of the Maine Maritime Academy
as a substitute for the *State of
Maine,* which had been sold to be
broken up.

1/3 The US Navy transports Barrett
(1), Geiger *(2) and* Upshur *(3) were
launched for American President Lines
as passenger ships of the standard
P2-S1-DN1 class.*

Periodicals

Germanischer Lloyd, Register (Berlin, Hamburg) from 1920
Jane's Fighting Ships (London) from 1938
Lloyd's Register of Shipping (London) from 1920
Weyer's Taschenbuch der Kriegsflotten (Munich) from 1935

Magazines

Die Seekiste (Kiel) 1950-1964
Engineering (London) 1930-1939
International Marine Engineering (New York) 1930-1935
Marine News (Kendal) 1950-1973
Schiffbau (Berlin) 1930-1939
Sea Breezes (Liverpool) 1949-1973
Shipbuilding and Shipping Record (London) 1928-1972
The Belgian Shiplover (Brussels) 1959-1973
The Motor Ship (London) 1928-1939
The Shipbuilder (London and Newcastle) 1930-1937

Books

Anderson, *White Star* (Prescot) 1964
Bonsor, *North Atlantic Seaway* (Prescot) 1955
de Boer, *The Centenary of the Stoomvaart Maatschappij 'Nederland' 1870-1970* (Kendal) 1970
Dictionary of American Naval Fighting Ships (Washington) Vols I-V
Dunn, *Passenger Liners* (Southampton) 1961
Emmons, *Pacific Liners 1927-1972* (Newton Abbot) 1973
Hocking, *Dictionary of Disasters at Sea during the Age of Steam* (London) 1969
Isherwood, *Steamers of the Past* (Liverpool)
Jentschura-Jung-Mickel, *Die japanischen Kriegsschiffe 1869-1945* (Munich) 1970
Kludas, *Die grossen deutschen Passagierschiffe* (Oldenburg and Hamburg) 1971
Maber, *North Star to Southern Cross* (Prescot) 1967
Musk, *Canadian Pacific* (London) 1968
Rohwer, *Die U-Boot-Erfolge de*

Achsenmächte 1939-1945 (Munich) 1968
Rohwer-Hümmelchen, *Chronik des Seekrieges 1939-1945* (Oldenburg and Hamburg) 1968
Smith, *Passenger Ships of the World* (Boston) 1963
Worker, *The World's Passenger Ships* (London) 1967

Other sources

Archives and publications of shipyards and shipping lines; statements and reports in newspapers.

I should like to register my very sincere thanks for the kind loan of photographs. The pictures in this book were obtained from the following sources:

American President Lines, San Francisco, page 155/2
Marius Bar, Toulon, pages 18/8, 29/3
Blohm & Voss AG, Hamburg, pages 23/1, 33/1, 36/1, 37/2 & 3, 48/1 & 2, 86/1 & 2, 87/3
Dr Paul Bois, Toulon, page 23/2
P.C. Brandwijk, Maassluis, pages 27/1, 67/2, 143/2, 171/1, 174/1, 187/1 & 2, 211/4
Frank O. Brayndard, Sea Cliff NY, pages 93/1 & 2, 94/1, 95/2 & 3, 96/4, 97/5, 98/7, 99/9, 101/10, 102/12, 103/13 & 14, 104/15, 105/16 & 17, 107/19 & 20, 109/21 & 22, 113/26 & 27, 114/1, 116/4, 123/11 & 12, 125/1 & 2, 127/4, 128/5, 129/7, 130/8, 131/10, 133/2, 135/3 & 4, 137/5 & 6, 141/8 & 9, 149/1 & 2, 230/1, 231/2
Cie Maritime Belge, Antwerp, page 181/5
Deutsche Luftbild KG, Hamburg, page 47/2
Deutsche Presse Agentur, Frankfurt, page 67/3
A. Duncan, Gravesend, pages 11/2, 17/7, 31/5, 37/4, 39/6, 41/2, 45/3, 58/1, 65/4, 69/1, 71/3, 91/1, 92/3, 145/1, 153/4, 155/1, 161/2, 163/1, 164/1, 169/4, 175/2, 185/2, 193/2 & 4, 197/7, 205/6, 217/3, 225/11, 228/1, 229/2
Laurence Dunn, Richmond, pages 61/4, 63/2, 163/4, 181/6

Ellerman Lines Ltd, London, page 26/1
Hans Graf, Hamburg, pages 19/11, 53/5, 63/1, 77/1, 133/1, 184/1, 215/1, 219/5 & 6, 221/8, 227/13
Fritz Hamann, Hamburg, page 35/4
Hapag-Lloyd AG, Hamburg and Bremen, page 88/4 & 5
Hans Hartz, Hamburg, pages 24/3, 35/3
F.W. Hawks, Rainham, page 55/1
Howaldtswerke-Deutsche Werft AG, Hamburg and Kiel, page 44/1
Imperial War Museum, London, page 13/3
C. Jansen, Hamburg, page 59/2
Rudie Kleyn, Voorburg, pages 27/2, 41/1, 65/3, 85/3, 151/1, 152/3, 167/2, 173/3, 179/1, 189/4, 202/1, 204/5
J.F. Horst Koenig, Hamburg, page 213/1
Achiv Lachmund, Hamburg, page 45/2
K.P. Lewis, Bromborough, pages 145/2, 192/1
Ian G.B. Lovie, Wellington, pages 56/1, 172/1, 195/6, 199/2, 209/2 & 3 211/5
H.J. Mayburg, Bremen, pages 119/7, 127/3, 131/9, 227/14
Messageries Maritimes, Marseille, page 143/1
National Archives, Washington, page 25/5
F. van Otterdijk, Hoboken, pages 75/3, 161/1, 173/2, 179/2
Pacific Steam Navigation Co, London, page 191/1 & 2
Peninsular and Oriental Steam Navigation Co, London, pages 9/1 & 2, 49/1 & 2, 165/3, 188/3, 189/5, 208/1
J.F. van Puyvelde, Brussels, pages 73/1 & 2, 176/3, 180/3, 183/7, 193/3, 195/5, 198/1, 217/4
H.-J. Reinecke, Hamburg, pages 77/2, 129/6, 200/4, 201/6, 203/3
Rotterdamsche Lloyd, Rotterdam, pages 146/1, 156/1, 157/2
K.-H. Schwadtke, Berlin, pages 33/2, 83/6, 231/3
Photo-Schemkes, Bremerhaven, page 46/1
Shaw, Savill & Albion Co Ltd, London, pages 54/1, 151/2

Paul H. Silverstone, New York, pages
97/6, 99/8, 101/11, 106/18,
111/23 & 24, 112/25, 115/2 & 3,
117/5 & 6, 120/9, 139/7
Skyfotos, Ashford Airport, Kent, page
74/1
Stoomvaart My 'Nederland',
Amsterdam, page 60/1 & 2
Svenska Amerika Linjen, Göteborg,
page 159/1
United States Lines Inc, New York,
pages 84/1, 85/2
Wilton-Fijenoord NV, Schiedam, page
29/4

All other photographs are from the
author's collection.